MW00379025

PRAISE FOR *WHAT GOES UNSPOKEN*

"Krystal Hardy Allen's book, *What Goes Unspoken*, is a must-read! She goes beyond theory into showing school leaders how to operationalize one of the most critical aspects of any school's success—diversity, equity, and inclusion. Principals and heads of school will not only learn how to do self-work, but they will also be able to measure their school's DEI efforts and help usher in checks and balances that foster engagement, sense of belonging, and the necessary environment for students, teachers, and staff to thrive."

—**Janice K. Jackson,** EdD, chief executive officer, Hope Chicago.
Former Superintendent of Chicago Public Schools.

"Diversity and equity are critical components in creating an inclusive and welcoming environment in any organization or community. Feeling accepted, valued, and recognized as part of the community is a basic need for all humans. *What Goes Unspoken* guides educational organizations as they begin to understand how to systematically create a culture of acceptance, empathy, and opportunities for all."

—**Geri Gillespy**, EdD, education industry executive, StraightUpEDU

What Goes Unspoken

How School Leaders Address DEI Beyond Race

KRYSTAL HARDY ALLEN

JOSSEY-BASS™
A Wiley Brand

Copyright © 2024 by Jossey-Bass Publishing. All rights reserved.

Published by John Wiley & Sons, Inc., Hoboken, New Jersey.
Published simultaneously in Canada.

No part of this publication may be reproduced, stored in a retrieval system, or transmitted in any form or by any means, electronic, mechanical, photocopying, recording, scanning, or otherwise, except as permitted under Section 107 or 108 of the 1976 United States Copyright Act, without either the prior written permission of the Publisher, or authorization through payment of the appropriate per-copy fee to the Copyright Clearance Center, Inc., 222 Rosewood Drive, Danvers, MA 01923, (978) 750-8400, fax (978) 750-4470, or on the web at www .copyright.com. Requests to the Publisher for permission should be addressed to the Permissions Department, John Wiley & Sons, Inc., 111 River Street, Hoboken, NJ 07030, (201) 748-6011, fax (201) 748-6008, or online at http://www.wiley.com/go/permission.

Trademarks: Wiley and the Wiley logo are trademarks or registered trademarks of John Wiley & Sons, Inc. and/ or its affiliates in the United States and other countries and may not be used without written permission. All other trademarks are the property of their respective owners. John Wiley & Sons, Inc. is not associated with any product or vendor mentioned in this book.

Limit of Liability/Disclaimer of Warranty: While the publisher and author have used their best efforts in preparing this book, they make no representations or warranties with respect to the accuracy or completeness of the contents of this book and specifically disclaim any implied warranties of merchantability or fitness for a particular purpose. No warranty may be created or extended by sales representatives or written sales materials. The advice and strategies contained herein may not be suitable for your situation. You should consult with a professional where appropriate. Further, readers should be aware that websites listed in this work may have changed or disappeared between when this work was written and when it is read. Neither the publisher nor authors shall be liable for any loss of profit or any other commercial damages, including but not limited to special, incidental, consequential, or other damages.

For general information on our other products and services or for technical support, please contact our Customer Care Department within the United States at (800) 762-2974, outside the United States at (317) 572-3993 or fax (317) 572-4002.

Wiley also publishes its books in a variety of electronic formats. Some content that appears in print may not be available in electronic formats. For more information about Wiley products, visit our web site at www.wiley .com.

Library of Congress Cataloging-in-Publication Data is Available:

ISBN 9781394163182 (Paperback)
ISBN 9781394163199 (ePDF)
ISBN 9781394163205 (ePUB)

Cover Design: Wiley
Cover Image: © melitas/Shutterstock
Author Photo: © Michael Moorer

SKY10053160_081423

I dedicate this book to my grandmothers. My siblings and I affectionately called my paternal grandmother "Grandma Toot"; however, her real name was Mamie Lee Hardy. Born in 1928 in Alabama's Black Belt, my grandmother was a sweet, caring, and hardworking Black woman who was also illiterate as she had only a first-grade education. Instead of finishing school, she helped her family via picking cotton and engaging in domestic housework for decades in every ounce of the worst conditions in the Jim Crow South. I remember going to doctor appointments with her and signing her names on the books to check in. She passed away in 2010 at the age of 82 years old, and there's not a day that goes by that I don't think about the symbolism of being her grandchild and how I am the walking embodiment of her dreams, hopes, and prayers.

My maternal grandmother, Janie Mae Sanders, still walks this earth as one of the most beautiful and wisest people I know. Born in 1939, she is a high school graduate who also engaged in domestic work and then was trained on the job to become a pharmacy technician by my hometown's only Black-owned pharmacist, the late Dr. Joseph Carstarphen. My grandmother has served as a friendly beacon of light to many families in Selma, Alabama, for decades in her faithful service as a pharmacy technician and devout member of her church community. I've always aspired to be generous to others, work hard, and allow my faith to be my lamp in this world the way she does.

I dedicate this book to these two women because they both represent the essence, nuance, beauty, and pain of Black womanhood over centuries, and they paved the way for me to be where I am today. This first book symbolizes—in the words of artist Brandon Odoms—just how much I am my ancestors' wildest dreams. I love and miss you, Grandma Toot. Grandma Janie, you are my rock.

Contents

Introduction

"Do the best you can until you know better. Then when you know better, do better."

—Maya Angelou

Whether you are a principal, a teacher, a superintendent, an instructional coach, a school board member, an education advocate, a parent, or any other form of educational leader or practitioner, this book is for you. In a sea of diversity, equity, and inclusion (DEI) dialogue and discourse, this book bridges the gap between theory and action by providing insights into the intrapersonal or inner work necessary for educators to center and advance DEI in a very real way, but it also provides concrete guidance on what centering and advancing DEI across multiple facets of education actually looks like and how to do it. This nexus of engagement in the internal work necessary for the journey, as well as a layout of the *how*, is so vital within the current climate of often heated, political debates over curriculum, athletic policies, school discipline, student safety, and more. As a former award-winning principal and teacher and now as a full-time education and management consultant, I cannot tell you how many educators I have met across the United States and abroad who philosophically agree that diversity matters, that inclusion is important, and that equity is right, but they do not often know how to actualize it in practice day-to-day. These educators may understand the *what*, but don't know the *how*. If you are one of those educators or educational leaders, this book will unlock clarity on the *how*.

I also meet educators and educational leaders who understand the *what* of DEI, know the *how* in terms of instruction and student culture and climate, but they have not actualized making their DEI holistic or more multifaceted outside of the student experience. For instance, their DEI efforts do not address what their commitment to DEI entails, what their policies are, what their mindsets and beliefs are, or what practices they enact that center and advance DEI within human resources, school or district finance, family and community engagement, school or district operations, and many more facets of what running a school, operating a school district, or leading an education-adjacent organization—such as education nonprofits—entail. In this regard, it is very possible that a teacher, a school, a district, or an education nonprofit spends time advocating for the just treatment of students, but doesn't thoughtfully do the same for adults within its care.

Do I meet educators and educational leaders who are resistant to understanding and embracing DEI? Absolutely. However, this book is not intended for that audience, but rather for the ones who genuinely want to learn how to make DEI real, actionable, or operationalized within the classrooms, schools, systems, and organizations they work within every day. Within this text, I share not only my subject matter expertise but also lived experiences from my own journey as a first-generation college graduate, a Black female educator, an educational leader, a charter school board member, an education consultant, an education advocate and philanthropist, and also a governing member of various education nonprofit boards.

As a native of historic Selma, Alabama, growing up in a space where discourse of social justice advocacy and activism was as normal for me as learning how to read a map, was a pointed experience. Often, I tell people that being from Selma is a salient part of my identity and how I show up in spaces because I feel that the convictions, beliefs, hopes, dreams, and potential in that space run through my veins. I am who I am because I was born in that space, to the community, to the people who are there, and to all the history that is there.

It is my hope that you are enlightened, encouraged, inspired, pushed, convicted, but, most important, equipped to engage in work that will not only change the lives of your students and team but also transform your own life by shifting the way you see, think about, and approach this topic forevermore. As an educator, systems leader, nonprofit leader, policy maker, or social entrepreneur, what are your hopes for your own journey of seeking to deepen your knowledge and understanding of DEI? What are you hoping to achieve in this next chapter of centering and advancing DEI as a leader or practitioner?

Key Point
The work of centering and advancing DEI is a lifelong journey and one we all must take in positioning ourselves to continue learning and unlearning.

WHY I WROTE THIS BOOK

"The paradox of education is precisely this—that as one begins to become conscious, one begins to examine the society in which he is being educated."

—James Baldwin

The year 2020 will always be etched within our minds as one of the most unforgettable moments in our lifetimes. The onset and spread of COVID-19 brought about the abrupt closure of schools, businesses, and more. Additionally, the loss of life, the pivots we all had to make to operate in a more virtual world, the fear and anxiety of the unknown, and the constant regulations on what we could and could not do transformed life as we all knew it. I can remember the lockdown as clear as yesterday. At the time, my husband and I were glued to the television daily in what felt like a true twilight zone, wiping down boxes and packages we received in the mail as no one fully knew at that time how you could contract COVID, and feeling anxiety and frustration at times with every new update and change we learned.

In the midst of this, racial tensions that were already brewing prior to COVID across the United States rose amidst continuous blatant, overt, and also even the most subtle acts of racism. Many communities of color—no different than times past—grew to a place of absolute disgust, fatigue, righteous anger, sadness, and frustration witnessing these acts happen over and over with little to no accountability and justice. This context is important to understand in order to then understand the outrage felt by many with the murder of George Floyd as well as the subsequent protests, petitions, and other expressions of pursuit of applying pressure and demands for change, particularly to and for Black and Brown communities across our nation.

As a result, many companies, nonprofit organizations, and individuals—particularly white people and predominantly white-led institutions—underwent what many have named as a racial reckoning. This entailed everything from making social media posts of public statements sharing how much they support DEI to organizations making posts of blank black squares to demonstrate solidarity with African Americans in light of blatant acts of police brutality to organizations investing thousands of dollars into anti-bias, cultural competency, and anti-racism trainings to companies kickstarting major philanthropic giving efforts and support programs for Black and Brown businesses.

In the midst of all of this, the education sector navigated its own interesting combination of reckoning and also resistance. Within the realm of education, the murder of George Floyd pushed numerous schools, school systems, and education-adjacent organizations to consider what their commitment was or should be toward racial DEI in particular. It also pushed some schools, school systems, and education-adjacent organizations to revisit what was their existing stated commitment to gauge whether it was legitimately what they were living out or whether it was simply a monument of symbolism that speaks to their espoused values (not their actual ones in practice). For other schools, school systems, and education nonprofits, the racial tensions that heightened during the pandemic resulted in organized efforts to ban any efforts that promoted DEI, such as banning books that highlight the holistic history of communities of color and paint white people in a light that some would prefer to erase, or restricting anything seen as culturally responsive. I'll never forget preparing to give a full day of customized professional development training within the state of South Carolina during the pandemic and being told to switch my language less than two weeks prior to our training, from using the term *equity* to anything else that could still address what our session objectives were because the word *equity* within that particular district and city was now seen as controversial, divisive, and inflammatory.

As you can see, the reaction to embracing DEI was and has been just as mixed within the education sector as it has been within other professional contexts or sectors. Prior to the unfortunate and traumatizing murder of George Floyd, many K–12 public school systems, as well as private schools, only moderately and often casually offered cultural competency trainings to teachers, school leaders, and noninstructional school staff members as a means of gently acknowledging difference and the need to be responsive to the array of students, families, and communities their systems served.

Nonetheless, for schools, systems, and education-adjacent organizations that did want to take steps toward creating more diverse, equitable, and inclusive schools, as well as non-education entities such as major business corporations many of us know and love, the first place many of them gravitated toward was the provision of training(s). For many, the thinking was aligned to a belief that hiring an external trainer (or in some cases providing internal professional development of some type) would fit the bill in order to prevent any overt acts of racism that could take place within workplace environments or for schools within classrooms. Unfortunately, for many schools, school systems, and education-adjacent organizations, their efforts only scratched the surface of what is truly needed to create a deeply diverse, inclusive, and equitable environment for not only children but adults alike.

Some trainings and resources address race exclusively, which is necessary as all discourse must center race, and there is no way we should discuss power, privilege, injustice, and more without centering race. Many educators are left in the dark as it pertains to understanding what DEI work that addresses other aspects of identity looks like or entails. This includes preparation and guidance on navigating matters of gender, neurodiversity, sexuality, mental health, socioeconomics (i.e., especially poverty), religion, and more. In this way, it is important to note that while we build educators and educational leaders' prowess to teach and lead for racial DEI, it must not occur at the cost of ignoring, perpetuating, or giving silent permission to allow for other forms of harm, injustice, and oppression students as well as adult educators feel and face.

Therefore, this text does two things in approach. It centers both race and other forms of identity, which Dr. Kimberlé Crenshaw coined as *intersectionality* within the 1980s. By no means does this mean that race should be ignored or dismissed as an excuse for a school, school system, or education-adjacent organization to skip, evade, or skirt around its racial work, but this names the need for an organization to examine its racial roots, needs, and work first and foremost while giving itself permission to expand its work over time so that the work it does also speaks to the reality of, for instance, Black children not only being Black as a monolithic being but also being multidimensional in who they are and how we should also see them, love them, support them, push them, and empower them to actualize their full potential and greatness.

Moreover, some trainings are comprehensive in approaching DEI work from the lens of multiple identities, but they only focus on students' academic learning experiences, student culture and climate, or family/community engagement; they fail to support and guide other educational leaders and stakeholders in also acknowledging and addressing the way that DEI should be implemented in other aspects of the school, district, or organization (for-profit or nonprofit), such as finance and development. This means that the work sends a message that DEI matters for the work with and for children and families, but it will not address the very real forms of interpersonal, institutional, and systemic harm, injustice, and oppression teachers themselves face, administrators face, noninstructional staff face, and more. There is not a day of my life that goes by in which I'm not thinking of and mindful of the fact that my own now successful education and management consulting firm started as a result of overt and subtle acts of nepotism, imbalanced support and accountability, and racism as a Black woman principal of a charter school within the at-will state of Louisiana.

Last but not least, sometimes DEI work within the education sector can fall short in its ability to build mostly conceptual or theoretical understanding, but unsuccessfully, ineffectively, or rarely addressing the concrete, practical work and steps necessary to not only center DEI but also advance it within classrooms, schools at large, and districts as a whole. There are perhaps very few educators in this world who set out to fail children, but unfortunately when we don't love, nurture, protect, and create transformational environments for children to learn and grow, to discover who they are, to be affirmed, and to be set up for holistic success, we do precisely that. True success for children is not piecemeal or monolithically designated and attached to their academic achievement. True success encompasses the psychological, emotional, social, physical, and even spiritual development of our young people. Doing such helps children not only excel academically but also become well-rounded people who know and love their identity, can discover who they are, fall in love with who they are, be themselves, and actualize their full potential, gifts, and talents.

As "K–12 DEI professional development has been under attack by conservative politicians who argue that the trainings are ineffective, divisive, and are meant to shame white people for something they are not responsible for" and "at least 14 states have passed laws restricting what schools can say and do in these trainings" (Najarro, 2022), this book teaches educational leaders across public and private schools how to shift from theory to action in operationalizing DEI within specific domains of school leadership and district operations. It also addresses the very important inner or intrapersonal work all school and educational systems leaders need to first address within themselves in order to champion work of this nature and ensure their work isn't performative, short-sighted, and, most important, ineffective.

Given this context, I'd love you to take the time to reflect on the questions you'll find throughout this text. I have allotted space and pages for you to jot your responses and use this information to inform how you move forward.

Key Point

Define and name your *why*. What leads you to engage in this work matters.

REFLECTION QUESTIONS

What is your organization's background or history as it pertains to its DEI journey? Has DEI been explicitly named as an organizational priority within your school, system, nonprofit, or company?

_____
_____
_____
_____
_____

Is this a new or newer journey for your organization, or have you already embarked on your journey? If the latter, have your efforts been fruitful, effective, and/or sustaining? Or is your organization's work rather performative, limited, and/or low impact?

_____
_____
_____
_____
_____

One

Getting Started

In Part 1, we will lay the vital groundwork to help you understand the prerequisites and ongoing work needed prior to making changes within practices and policies. It is important to ensure that we are on a committed journey of doing our own individual inner work and ensuring that our teams are engaged in intrapersonal work as well so that our efforts to make changes are not performative, short-lived, or fall flat because we lack the mindsets, beliefs, and dispositions to engage in and sustain the real work and change necessary to center and advance DEI.

CHAPTER 1

Establishing a Shared Language and Vision

"If you change the way you look at things, the things you look at change."

—Wayne Dyer

Now before we move forward, let's norm the very three words all of this text is centered on: *diversity*, *equity*, and *inclusion*. At this moment in our country and around the world, the words *diversity*, *equity*, and *inclusion* have quickly become buzzwords within organizations, media, politics, and beyond. They can be words that are simply tossed about for a variety of reasons. For some leaders, they are words—any individual word or all three words—that are used intentionally to drive a public or outward stance that they or their school, district, network, nonprofit, or company believes in, cares about, or seeks to champion for a more diverse, equitable, and inclusive educational ecosystem and reality for students, families, their staff members, and our world.

For other leaders, those words are used to uphold a political, economic, faith-based, or other type of agenda they or their organization are committed to driving as a leader. Some leaders point to these words as being divisive, controversial, and problematic terms. Motives, intentions, and uses of the words *diversity*, *equity*, and *inclusion* truly vary across geographies, schools, and educational system types, and more. Nonetheless, one thing is true: the way you define words matters, and thus this first chapter is dedicated to first helping you understand what these words mean and also expanding your understanding of what these terms mean, and why that expansion matters.

DIVERSITY

Before diving into this first term, I would love to know how you currently think of diversity. When you hear the word *diversity*, what is the first thing that comes to your mind? What is diversity to you? Within this text as well as within my firm's work supporting the education sector (i.e., early childhood centers, K–12 schools, education nonprofits, colleges and universities, education tech companies, etc.), I define *diversity* as representation across the board or, in other words, it is a variety of areas of identity or difference. This definition is very important to note because far too often the word *diversity* is used as a synonym for race and ethnicity. It's common, for instance, to hear a company leader note that they've made a diversity hire, and in this case, they are usually speaking to having hired a person of color. It is also commonplace to hear a parent speak to the fact that their child attends a very diverse school, and by this, they are often referring to their child attending a school that is racially and/or ethnically diverse. Last but not least, another example would be hearing someone speak to the notion of their school or school system having a diversity issue, and often by it they mean that their school or school system may be experiencing tensions, conflicts, or challenges that are racially driven in some manner. Consider the way that many media outlets speak about the word *diversity*: they are often connecting it to topics, headlines, and storylines that are in some way centering race.

Is race diversity? Yes. However, diversity isn't just about race. Diversity is actually a broad undertaking of consideration of many different types of identity, representation, and difference, so it's important to know that we have to name precisely and specifically what types of diversity we as individuals, we as schools, we as school systems, we as nonprofits, and we as education companies we are speaking of, focusing on, and centering (see Figure 1.1).

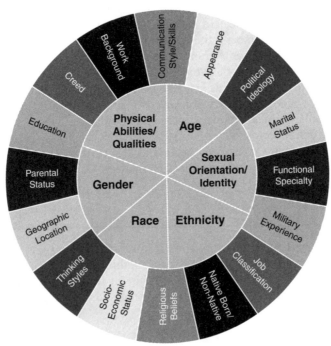

FIGURE 1.1 Social identity wheel.
Source: Medical Group Medical Association.

In the following list, you'll find examples of other forms and types of diversity that exist and also represent who are our students are, who our families are, who our communities are, and who we are as educators ourselves:

- **Racial/ethnic diversity.** Examples include but are not limited to mindfulness of Black, Latino, Asian-American, Pacific Islander, Indigenous, and more racial and ethnic communities of students, families, staff members, and stakeholders.
- **Gender diversity.** Examples include but are not limited to males (men and boys), females (women and girls), cisgendered, gender fluid, gender non-conforming, and other gender categories that our students, your colleagues, students' families, and other stakeholders identify as.
- **Neurodiversity.** Examples of neurodivergence include but are not limited to students and adults with autism, attention deficit/hyperactivity disorder (ADHD), dyslexia, dysgraphia, and more.
- **Diversity within socioeconomic background.** Examples include but are not limited to students, families, colleagues, and other stakeholders from low-income backgrounds, which is also divided between those who simply draw from low or lower wages or salaries versus individuals who live extremely below the poverty line. Diversity within socioeconomic background also includes individuals from middle-class or -income backgrounds, which isn't a monolithic group, either, similar to the aforementioned example of individuals—especially students—of lower income background.
- **Diversity of sexuality/sexual orientation.** Examples include but are not limited to individuals who are heterosexual, bisexual, asexual, pansexual, and other sexual orientations our students, we ourselves, our colleagues, families, and other stakeholders identify as.
- **Diversity within family background.** Examples include but are not limited to grandparent-led households, households of same-sex marriages, so for students this might translate to but not be limited to two moms or two dads being present at home, foster families, adopted families, and more.

Although what is listed here is in no way exhaustive, it does go to show that there are many aspects and dimensions of diversity that can be found within the work we do every day as educators. In no way will you ever be mindful of 50 million types of diversity as you move about your day teaching students, leading campuses, managing organizations, and leading systems, but the goal is that you understand that diversity is deeper than race.

Diversity is and speaks to the wide variety of forms of representation. Truly the importance is ensuring that you carry consideration for multiple perspectives, viewpoints, lived experiences, backgrounds, voices, and needs in what you say and do in your work each and every day. When you push for diversity, push for centering race and racial/ethnic diversity in what you're doing, but also make sure you're mindful of other aspects of diversity our students, families, colleagues, and stakeholders embody so that we do not embrace just one aspect of who they are. We want to make room for other aspects of our students' and even adults' identities as well.

When you think about your daily work, as an educator or educational leader, there are some aspects of diversity you may already be incredibly conscious of as well as intentional about centering within your work.

REFLECTION QUESTIONS

What are the types of diversity you're most conscious of and intentional about within your work?

What are the types of diversity you're not as mindful of, intentional about centering, or have blind spots about?

Conversely, there are types of diversity that may rarely or ever cross your mind as a teacher, noninstructional staff member within a school, school administrator, nonprofit organizational leader, or leader of an education-based company. Because you do not think of these things on a day-to-day basis, this doesn't automatically make you evil, bigoted, or harmful, but rather it makes you human because there is not one human being that holds absolutely every single type of diversity there is within their minds, words, and actions at all times. All of us—and I do mean all of us, including educators and educational leaders of color—have blind spots or things that are not at the very forefront of your thinking, your decision-making, and your actions everyday as you interact and engage with colleagues, serve students, and engage families.

As human beings, we often are most conscious and intentional about aspects or types of diversity that we are most proximate (or close) to or aspects and types of diversity that speak to our own lived experiences. What does this mean? It means that we tend to think of the aspects and types of diversity that connect to the shoes we walk in every day, as well as the aspects and types of diversity that hit close or closest to home.

As a Black woman who is also a person of faith; a native of historic Selma, Alabama; and a first-generation college graduate from a lower socioeconomic background, the following types of diversity are often at the forefront of my mind within any and every space I occupy:

- Race/ethnicity
- Gender
- Income and class
- Religion
- Geography

This doesn't mean that other types of diversity are of lesser value to me, but it does mean that I—for instance—am hyper-aware of, super-intentional about centering, and constantly advocating for the following:

- **Racial diversity of students, educators, board members, families, and other stakeholders.** For example, I want to ensure that not only Black students see representation within curriculum, school programming, and guest speakers but also that we are having conversations about other students of color who aren't Black but are members of our school communities. We often use the phrase "Black and Brown," but in some spaces students who are considered "Brown" (e.g., Latino, Indigenous, etc.) are a complete afterthought. If our Black students develop empowerment and pride as to who they are and what they can be, we must ensure that all of our other students of color experience and feel the same. To what extent are Latino students within your school seeing themselves (and positively so) within the texts you leverage within your classroom or school? To what extent are Asian American students (as well as all of the other students within your school) able to experience meaningful programming that elevates and amplifies the beauty and power of Asian American heritage?
- **Consideration of gender diversity within the composition of decision-making bodies, such as school boards and school leadership teams.** For example, it's amazing how many school districts across our country hold gender bias against women for high school principal positions. Although the mind may nearly automatically go to the belief of this happening from male executive leaders (such as superintendents or a district's principal managers) toward female candidates for high school principal positions, this is not always the case. Whether the gatekeeper or key decision-maker within an interview process is a female, male, nonbinary, gender fluid, and so on leader, there is often a consistent belief that men can handle leadership of high school campuses as opposed to women. Women educators—no matter how many degrees they have, no matter how many certifications they hold, or how many years of exemplary experience they have—often experience difficulty obtaining those positions within some cities and towns across the country. This is unfortunate because this then means that some male candidates who are underqualified or unmatched to their female counterparts are

provided positions based on the fact that they are men and assumed to—within those settings—to be "stronger" or "better" disciplinarians, hold more executive presence, are listened to more and differently from staff teams as well as families, can diffuse conflict "better," and more. All of these things often trace back to the depth of our societal socialization of gender roles and expectations.

- **The implications of our work on families who are economically disadvantaged.** For example, it's important to consider accessibility for all parents and families within your school community. One thing that any educator or educational leader can take for granted, for instance, is transportation and the assumption that all parents and families have access to a car or another form of transportation to and from your school campus. Because this is not the case for all parents and families, it is very important to consider the ways that you and your school community can meet different parents where they are. This might include the purchase of bus tickets with additional unrestricted funds the school has at its disposal that can be used exclusively for parent-teacher conference days. This could also include hosting or offering parent-teacher conferences before school hours, during school hours, after school within the evenings, or offering night conferences to accommodate different parent, guardian, or family working schedules. Making the decision to host a parent-teacher conference event within the middle of the day, and making that one time the only option for parents to access makes a few short-sighted assumptions. One assumption is that all parents and families (who work or hold jobs) have the ability to take time off of their jobs via PTO (paid time off) opportunities. Some parents and families do not hold salaried positions, which means that when they take time off, it disproportionately affects their compensation. When they don't work (because their roles are hourly), they do not get paid, which means that certain needs cannot be met. Therefore, scheduling parent-teacher conferences with a morning option, a mid-day option, and perhaps even an evening offering for parents becomes a great way to model mindfulness of the diverse needs of the students as well as adults that we serve.

- **The dismantling of elitism within interactions and engagement between educators and families, particularly within early childhood and K–12 schools serving parents, guardians, and caregivers who are financially disadvantaged and less educated.** For example, you'd be shocked at the dynamics that sometimes play out between educators and educational leaders from middle-class backgrounds, as well as affluent backgrounds, and parents and families from lower socioeconomic backgrounds, particularly those who live in poverty, within early childhood as well as K–12 school settings that serve socioeconomically disadvantaged youth. There is often an assumption held by said educators and educational leaders that they know what is best for the children they serve, that the families are inferior due to their financial status and often lack of education or limited education, and that their parents and families are not capable of being thought partners and contributing decision-makers for their children's education. In some spaces, this means that educators not only believe they know best when it comes to what their students and families need but they also look down on them.

- **The psychological and emotional safety of students and adults within school spaces whose faith or religious denomination falls within the minority category of religious representation within their local context.** For example, as a person of faith, I grew up in a small Southern town in the late 1980s and early 1990s in which prayer took place in schools and everyone I knew was of Baptist denomination and attended Sunday church or worship services. In fact, as a kid and even early teen I didn't know that other denominations existed, as well as had no schema nor had ever heard of atheism. It wasn't until I left my hometown and attended a selective college preparatory residential high school—the Alabama School of Mathematics and Science—that I was exposed to religious diversity. For the first time in my life, I was surrounded not only by peers but also instructors and campus administrators who were of different faith backgrounds, such as Catholicism, Episcopalism, and Buddhism, as well as those who didn't believe in a higher power. That high school experience, as well as attending a Catholic university (the University of Notre Dame), made me hyper-aware of the ways in which a school environment can create not only acceptance but also a culture of learning and celebration of other faiths/faith backgrounds. How often in a public school setting is a teacher, noninstructional staff member, school leader, or district leader, who is also a person of faith, making statements with the assumption that those listening are also persons of faith? How often are staff members of a school made to feel uncomfortable because they're not even given the opportunity to opt in or out of a religious practice that may take place on a campus (essentially not providing room for volition to be exercised)? Similar to the way that we as educational leaders consider other aspects of diversity in creating psychologically and emotionally safe work environments for staff members, we must also be mindful of the religious diversity of the staff teams we lead and not make assumptions and take actions simply grounded in our own backgrounds as "the norm."
- **Adequate representation of heroes and success stories across geographic regions of the United States.** For example, within the education tech world, sometimes curricular initiatives highlight successful science, technology, engineering, and mathematics (STEM) trailblazers, notables, or leaders they believe students should know. Our firm recently noticed that the focus on STEM figures of color as well as gender diversity of the STEM figures was highlighted, but that each of the figures who were pointed out were all from major metropolitan areas and cities in every region of the United States, except the southeastern United States as a region as well as rural contexts in general. Though someone could consider this oversight small and that it might not matter, the truth is that it does. We send messages—even if they are unintentional—about who is worthy, what is notable, and what success looks like by whom we choose to highlight and whom we don't. The same thing holds to be true about where figures are from or reside. When we leave out an entire region of the United States repeatedly within our curricular spotlights, it sends and often—in this case—reinforces a stereotypical narrative of the southeastern United States that is not positive, but rather drenched in assumption of brilliance, intelligence, progression, or innovation not being found within this area of the country by way of its people and/or talent.

As you consider these examples of areas I'm very conscious that so far they are based on my own lived experiences, and I know that this means there are some areas of diversity I have to do intentional work in thinking about and centering because they are not at the forefront of my mind. A prime example of this would be consciousness of physical disabilities, such as the need for wheelchair accessibility. If you are reading this text and are an able-bodied individual who has the ability to walk freely like myself, that means the following:

- You didn't wake up thinking to yourself "Who is going to help me out of bed today?"
- You probably never have to wonder whether a building you need to venture to (for instance, your place of work) has an elevator or ramps for you to be able to access an event you're planning to attend.
- In planning an event, one of your top five planning questions may not center on whether the venue you've chosen is accessible to anyone who might be physically impaired.

Conversely, something I developed a heightened sense of awareness about over the years is military status, particularly of the parents, caregivers, or guardians who are active members of the military, and especially those who are deployed. I'm the oldest of three kids, and one of my siblings is a Marine. Years ago, he was on active duty within Iraq and then Afghanistan. While he was away, and as a person of faith, I would always pray for him and his protection being in such hostile and scary conditions. Whenever I would see a news broadcast of an explosion within those geographic territories of the world, I would be triggered emotionally to either tears at times or immediately driven to pray even more deeply for him. There are some people who would or could see the exact same news broadcast one morning, make a cup of coffee, and leave home moving about their day as they usually do every day. This doesn't mean that the person who is unphased by news of this broadcast is a bad, evil, or bigoted person toward people who actively serve within the military or toward military families, but it does mean that they may not be mindful of, conscious of, or intentional in thought about considerations for military-related matters. Now, let's think about this in relation to our work as educators.

Imagine a city that is a heavily military community and an elementary school within it provides annual Mother's Day activities for its students. You can nearly envision a plethora of arts and crafts that students can partake in, which may include glitter, scissors, construction paper, and more, all while creating something their mothers will cherish for a lifetime. Based on the context provided about this being a military-heavy community, it's important that teachers as well as administrators supplement their traditional Mother's Day activities for other options for students to engage in that acknowledges, respects, and honors the realities of these students:

- Those whose mothers are actively deployed (similar to what I described with my own brother)
- Those whose mothers are deceased
- Those who are adopted or currently living within foster families or homes

■ Those whose mothers—for a variety of reasons—are alive but do not raise or provide primary care to them, such as a student who is actively being raised by an aunt, their grandmother, or even a close friend of the family

Many possibilities could be true, but the one I want to focus on is the first bullet. Let's suppose that qualitative data revealed that 13% of the school's population were students whose mothers are actively deployed abroad. If that were the case, the provision of traditional Mother's Day activities could actually be psychologically and emotionally triggering for these students. Given this, administrators and teacher leaders may decide to not only offer the traditional craft options they usually do, but to also do the following:

■ Partner with a local university's social work and counseling department to provide in-kind or free and optional counseling or therapy sessions for students to take advantage in the event that they'd like to join other kids who may be navigating grief or loss of a mother or motherly figure.
■ Provide opportunities to write letters to mothers who are deployed.

Doing all three things—for instance—provides an example of how holding consciousness of a student or family's military duty status could make a tremendous difference in ensuring that a school community is also a powerful healing space for students. This level of consciousness may not be at the forefront of a teacher's or educational leader's mind if they themselves have never experienced being on active duty or have never been proximate to a family member or loved one or close friend who has been on active duty within the military or have lacked proximity and deep exposure to the lived realities of active duty military people. As an educator, when you learn that a parent, such as a mother, is not actively present within a child's life, do you ever consider deployment as one option or reality for your students, or does it never or rarely cross your mind?

REFLECTION QUESTIONS

> **Given what you've just read, what areas or types of diversity now come to mind where you are not as mindful of or intentional about centering within your work in the education sector?**

> **In the area(s) you've named, what do you feel compelled to do in order to be more conscious, mindful, and intentional in your thinking, decision-making, and actions/habits?**

Key Point

Diversity is not only race. Race is one type of diversity, and must be centered, but it is not the only form of identity our students, staff members, and community hold.

INCLUSION

Oftentimes, we've heard the idea that inclusion is about having a seat at the table. When you hear the word *inclusion*, what is the first thing that comes to your mind? What does *inclusion* mean to you? Whereas diversity is centering the question of representation, *inclusion* refers to the importance of paying attention to access to resources, opportunities, and power, as well as the quality of experiences our students, our families, educators, and staff members themselves, as well as other stakeholders or people, have. As mentioned, we've all heard the idea that inclusion is about having a seat at the table. However, it's far deeper than simply that. Inclusion speaks to the quality of experiences one faces.

In this regard, let's imagine a school system that has had really low representation of women in principalship and middle leadership positions within schools. Let's note that this district recognizes and sees this as a problem and genuinely desires to change this. This is a diversity matter because we are specifically speaking to a lack of representation of women within this scenario, but it is—remember—very important to note and call out what specific type of diversity the district is addressing in tackling this. Because it is exclusively targeting women, this makes it a matter of gender diversity.

Now, let's imagine that this school system addresses this challenge by consistently hiring more women over time. Although we can give the district credit for this move, we must also focus on inclusion, and recognize that diversity and inclusion are not the same things. Just because there are more women doesn't mean that those women experience an inclusive workplace environment. In order to center and drive inclusion, we must ask—for instance—to what extent do women within our school, district, network, nonprofit, or company experience the following:

- Feel seen?
- Feel valued and appreciated?
- Feel heard?
- Are psychologically and emotionally safe?
- Feel that they can be their full authentic selves?
- Ever experience being called *honey, sweetie, little girl, babe,* or other terms by their male counterparts?
- Have access to breastfeeding lactation rooms or spaces?
- Experience being credited for the ideas they contribute, solutions they drive, deliverables they create, and more?
- Experience being often cut off or interrupted when they speak or are attempting to verbally express their thoughts?
- Receive promotions at a rate that is comparable to their male counterparts within the school, district, network, nonprofit, or company?
- Are fairly compensated or paid as well as their male counterparts?

These are only a sample of the questions that speak to whether the district is truly an inclusive environment for women. They demonstrate just how much having a seat at the table is not enough, but rather examine people's actual experience when they're there. What good is it to provide anyone—in this example, women—a seat at a table where they're disrespected, disregarded, overlooked, or not treated well? This is why we must ensure that our work in driving representation within schools and the education sector in general is not simply about ensuring that we have representation of different students of color, different teachers of color, different leaders of color within our work, but that our students of color, teachers of color, and leaders of color—for instance—are also being treated right and experiencing what they deserve—respect, dignity, psychological safety, emotional safety, and more.

We shouldn't simply applaud the increase of educators who are natives of a city where a charter school network is located and doesn't have a historic pattern of hiring natives if we are not also examining the experiences those natives have within that charter school network. We shouldn't rest our laurels on the integration of artwork throughout school displaying and celebrating the heritages of Asian American/Pacific Islander students if we are not also committed to examining the actual lived experiences our Asian American/Pacific Islander students are having within our care, within our schools.

Key Point

Inclusion is far deeper than having a seat at the table. It doesn't matter if I have a seat if am not treated properly when I'm there. If I am not respected, valued, appreciated, or heard, this is a table where I have been invited to be a token.

EQUITY

When you hear the word *equity*, what is the first thing that comes to your mind? What is *equity* or what does it mean to you? As diversity centers representation and inclusion speaks to the quality of experiences that students, staff members, families, and other stakeholders have, *equity* is a two-fold examination of access and differentiation that is or is not taking place within a school, education nonprofit, or education company, as well as an examination of outcomes we see with students, staff members, families, and other stakeholder our education sector serves.

So, let's first break down what I mean by access and differentiation. From the lens of access, equity speaks to the access persons have to power, resources, and opportunity within a space. We must essentially examine a person's or group's positionality within a space, such as a school, a district, a nonprofit, or a company. In the prior section on inclusion, I used an example of women and their lack of representation within a school district. Whereas increasing the number of women within a school district speaks truly to the district's work addressing gender diversity, any of the efforts that center the quality of experiences that these women have within a school district—from an access standpoint—must examine the following things:

- What roles do women (or any group or profile of students, staff members, families, or other stakeholders) occupy within our school district?
- Are women simply within junior or entry-level roles with our system?
- Are there any women within middle leadership roles within our district?
- Are there any women within senior leadership or executive roles within our school district?
- Are there any women on our board (of directors)?
- If we have underrepresentation of women, how do we integrate women intentionally throughout various functions of the organization?

All of these questions speak to the positionality that women in this case (or any group or profile of students, staff members, families, or other stakeholders) hold within a school, school district, education nonprofit organization, or an educational institution of any type. These questions matter because they speak to whether women hold real power, have any say, or even have the opportunity to influence the directionality or decisions made. If an educational leader isn't careful, we'll work really hard to have diverse and inclusive spaces, but not ever initiate conversations about whether a group or profile of individuals have adequate access to exercise leadership, power, or voice.

And it doesn't stop there. Equity also speaks to the access that our students, families, staff members, and other stakeholders have to the resources they need to be successful and thrive. Within our work educating kids, if a student were blind, we'd understand the importance of that student having access to braille in order to be able to read; that provision is an example of equity in action. This thinking must also extend to many other aspects of our work.

We must—for instance—ask ourselves the following as we apply an equity lens within our school, district, network, nonprofit, or company:

- What resources and supports do our students who are socioeconomically disadvantaged need that are within our locus of control of being able to provide? Have we identified those things, and do we provide them access to such?
- What resources and supports do our students who are learning English as a second language need in order to thrive within our classrooms? Do we or have we allotted the time, effort, and resources to provide them access with what they need?
- What resources and supports do our first-year and early career teachers need to be truly set up for success within the classroom? Do we give them what they need?
- What resources and supports do our teachers of color need in order to feel a sense of belonging within our organization? Are we willing to even have the conversation to acknowledge that their experiences may be different than their white counterparts?

All of these questions are examples, but they all speak to whether we are willing to differentiate what we do in order to meet people where they are and give them what they need to succeed, excel, thrive, and, honestly, to level the playing field—particularly when we are expecting students, families, staff members, and other stakeholders to meet the same outcomes and destinations of individuals who have many things (privilege) working in their favor.

My mind automatically goes to thinking about the pandemic and many of the unfortunate inequities that were not necessarily new, but were compounded, highlighted, and exposed in a very major way. One example of this would be the reality of Wi-Fi access, as well as overall access to laptops that students within rural communities often did not have. When we examine schools within the same state that have access in general to strong Wi-Fi connections, but also within their district's homes (which also speaks to socioeconomic or financial background status), and when we examine the schools where students have one-on-one access to their own laptops at school and/or at home provided by their districts, we must recognize that having access to Wi-Fi alone is a privilege that not all students have.

In this case, we also must recognize that for students within rural communities, there are areas of the state where there are no Wi-Fi towers, and thus, students do not have access to internet connection at all or their access is incredibly limited. For those students, the work of telecommunication communities such as Verizon or AT&T partnering with school systems and state, county, and local governments to install Wi-Fi towers and provide Wi-Fi hotspots became incredibly helpful in ensuring that when provided laptops to take home, those students could actually use them to submit assignments or simply attend school virtually. This type of partnership to drive parody within access to Wi-Fi connectivity is an example of an equity move. Equity is the assurance that individuals get what they need to function and thrive. In this case, equity looks like the assurance that students within rural communities are on a level playing field with students from urban communities across a state.

Even the provision of laptops to students, families, and school systems who prior to COVID didn't have access to them is an equity move in that it levels the playing field for students, families, and school systems to participate in digital learning like their peers who are able to do so given the mandate that learning switched to that particular platform.

Key Point
Equity is the practice of differentiating and attending to progress and results.

RECAP

Here is a recap or synopsis of ways you can think about these terms that help them become even more sticky for you along your journey:

- Diversity: representation
- Equity: access and differentiation (process) + outcomes (results)
- Inclusion: quality of experiences

REFLECTION QUESTIONS

How has your definition or the meaning you assigned to the term *diversity* changed as a result of what's been discussed in this chapter?

What is top of mind for you at this moment as you think about the diversity of your classroom, your school, your nonprofit, your institution, or your company? What types of diversity are present? What is not? What types of diversity are you most conscious of? What blind spots in regard to diversity are unearthed for you at this moment? In other words, what are you not as mindful of and would like to be more mindful of in relation to diversity moving forward?

How has your definition or the meaning you assigned to the term *inclusion* changed as a result of what's been discussed in this chapter?

What is top of mind for you at this moment as you think about the state of inclusion within your classroom, your school, your nonprofit, your institution, or your company for specific groups of students, staff members, parents/families, and other stakeholders you engage with or serve? Who do you believe is most seen, valued, heard, and/or appreciated within your classroom, school, nonprofit, institution, or company? Who is not? Who is psychologically and emotionally safe? Who is not? Who feels comfortable being their full authentic selves? Who might not? What profile of students, colleagues/staff members, parents/families/guardians, and others may have a more uneven, unfair, or challenging experience within your classroom, school, nonprofit, institution, or company?

CHAPTER 2

Looking in the Mirror

"I think it's important to hold a mirror up to society and yourself."

—Ricky Gervais

We all have blind spots. As a consultant who provides customized professional development workshops, I have always prided myself on being able to reach both the minds and the hearts of participants within a workshop or training setting. This begins from the moment participants enter the doors of the venue or space to the moment they leave the training they've just received. I carefully make eye contact with attendees, greet them with a smile, engage in genuine conversations to get to know folks in the room, and generally build positive rapport with them as I know that often some people enter spaces like this with all types of thoughts about what they're about to engage in. Some will enter thinking "I really don't want to be here." Some will enter thinking "This is going to be a waste of my time." Some even enter—especially when it's a DEI session—thinking "I have been to so many DEI training sessions. What more is there to cover?" My job as not only a facilitator but also a social justice advocate is to ensure that everyone in the room leaves feeling quite opposite than wherever they were in thoughts and feelings when they leave. The goal is to enlighten, to foster deep reflection, to challenge, to elevate awareness, and to spark concrete action.

That said, no matter how intentional I've been in my work, I still make mistakes and errors that connect very deeply to my own blind spots. Within one of my professional development training sessions, I kicked off by facilitating an icebreaker that asked participants to go back to their childhood or teen days and recall one of their celebrity crushes, then share it with a shoulder partner or someone who sat near them. As usual, I provided a minute of think time and then proceeded to have participants share their responses with each other. As I scanned the room while people were sharing, I could feel so much joy, I could hear laughter, and I simply knew at that moment that the session was off to a wonderful start. One and a half hours later when the workshop ended, I had a few participants stick around and provide very affirmative feedback on what they learned and how thankful they were for the content. However, the very last participant in line waiting to chat with me said—and I'll never forget her words—that she learned so much during the workshop and was grateful that she had attended and at the same time she wanted to give me feedback regarding something I had done that made her incredibly uncomfortable.

She went on to share to recount the icebreaker activity—the same one I thought was one of the highlights of the workshop in setting a really positive tone. She shared that when I provided the prompt of that question it gave her a sour feeling in her stomach and a sense of anxiety on the spot because the work environment of her peers in that particular workshop was one that was highly homophobic and not welcoming to members of the LGBTQ community, which she was a part of. She shared that she was lesbian, talked about how much she loves her wife, and how for the past 16 years, she has never disclosed to her coworkers that her partner was a woman because of the insensitive jokes some made about the LGBTQ community, and her knowing that had she disclosed her sexuality, it might cost her not only emotional discomfort but also forms of retaliation and discrimination within the workplace. That said, when I made this particular icebreaker question the sole question posed and made it mandatory that everyone share their responses with peers around them, it left her with no other choice than to participate in the activity itself. However, she shared that she made an intentional choice to lie and come up with a different crush who was of male gender just to blend in and provide herself cover within this exercise.

The fact that she had to do this was not okay, and I thus immediately apologized to her for not even being thoughtful of the blind spot of how a question of that nature could be an uncomfortable one for someone who was a member of the LGBTQ community. It was important for me to listen. It was important for me to seek to understand. It was also important for me to acknowledge my error and own it, not try to justify it by expressing how much I didn't mean to it. Instead, I made a choice to put emphasis on the impact of my action(s) instead of placing sole or an imbalanced emphasis on my intent. Impact matters more than intent. I had caused harm, and here I was teaching content of how to combat something, and in this moment, it reinforced not only my humanity but our humanity in the sense that DEI is lifelong work that requires nonstop learning and unlearning, as well as applying what we learn.

At that moment, I ended this learning opportunity by asking this session participant how to fix or address that particular icebreaker exercise. I asked if the question itself was bad or needed to be changed, and how it could be a better and a more inclusive question. She shared that the question in and of itself wasn't a bad question, and that she would have gladly and truthfully answered it in a different space. In that moment, I knew she meant in a space that provided her with both psychological and emotional safety. Her suggestion to me was to actually keep the icebreaker question, and instead of making it mandatory, simply add one to two more questions into the activity and provide the option for participants to answer any one question of their choice, which would automatically take the pressure off of anyone of feeling pigeonholed, nervous, psychologically or emotionally unsafe, and more, the way she had during the opening of our session. Hearing this idea, I graciously thanked her for this suggestion, and have implemented it year after year from that day on.

Although I recognize not only the formal training within DEI discourse I've engaged in for years but also what I've learned from lived experience and advocated for and modeled as a young adult, educator, and community advocate, that entire moment revealed a blatant blind spot I had for matters of gender as well as sexuality being a cisgendered woman and also a heterosexual one, particularly within the southeastern United States. As such, I have never had to consider whether a male crush I could name and share with peers would be met with strange stares, subsequent acts of malice, or fear of any form of retaliation in the workplace. No matter who my partner might be in a turn-and-talk activity within a professional development workshop, I to this day feel comfortable sharing openly and freely my celebrity crush, and because I feel comfortable, it can be easy for me to take for granted that not everyone feels or experiences this comfort, such freedom, and psychological safety to do the same. That, my friend, is an example of a blind spot in action, and demonstrates the things we can take for granted based on how we as individuals navigate the world each and every day.

Key Point

We all have work to do. Learning and unlearning is not signature of the responsibility of white educators and leaders but should be a priority for us all. Being a person of color or member of another marginalized group doesn't exempt you from the capability of perpetuating harm.

PEELING BACK THE LAYERS OF MINDSETS

We begin our work therefore looking into the mirror because it is easier to analyze and critique the actions of institutions and systems, which should be held accountable, but it must be met with the commitment to also critically examine oneself as well. In order to make true, enduring, and the most meaningful change, your journey of centering and advancing DEI must involve committing to do the work at the individual level (i.e., intrapersonal work or often what would be considered the "inner work"), the institutional level (i.e., which encompasses both your departmental or team-level work, as well as organization-wide efforts), and advocating for systemic change (i.e., macro-level changes across organizations and systems) as well.

It's quite easy to adopt a purely technical lens of DEI work as a leader. This might look like falling into the trap of believing that the adoption of a checklist or framework along with your team's fidelity and consistency in its use will drive your school or district to become a more inclusive environment, an embrace of diversity in its many forms, and provide equitable outcomes for children. This might also look like falling into the trap of believing that a singular DEI training or a series alone will address your need to center and advance DEI within your school, school system, or education-adjacent organization. Am I saying that checklists aren't effective? No. Am I saying that trainings are ineffective as a method of centering and advancing DEI? No again. Tools have their place and are important. In fact, as leaders, tools often help us to institutionalize practices within schools, districts, and education-adjacent organizations as a whole, but *there is no singular checklist, framework, or tool that can replace the inner work needed for the journey.*

The absolute best thing you can do as an educator is embrace the fact that the work of DEI must begin with *you.* You cannot advance an agenda that you are not willing to first examine at the *intrapersonal* level, which means that this work requires the courage to explore your own lens, schema, worldviews, socialization, bias, privilege, and shortcomings. I use the word *courage* intentionally because if you are an educator reading this text, you probably already care deeply for children, have an affinity to our profession, and consider yourself a good person. Yet, all of that can be true, and at the same time, you can participate in the perpetuation of a form of harm; the advancement of inequity in some way, shape, or form; or the process of making a child in your care or an adult you interface with—be it a parent, colleague, or external stakeholder to your school community—not feel seen, valued, heard, or appreciated. In other words, you can be a well-meaning educator and not *effectively* center DEI. The question isn't what are your intentions. The question is whether you are willing to examine how what you house inside—your mindsets, your beliefs, and your blind spots for instance—directly or indirectly affect others, namely, children and colleagues every day.

Here are actions that are often missteps:

- Resting on your laurels thinking that your school, nonprofit, or business is equitable, inclusive, anti-racist, psychologically and emotionally safe, and more *just* because of the high volume of Black or Brown staff members you have *or* because you have a Black or Brown leader
- Being in a school that is *incredibly* unsafe for LGBTQ+ youth (and coworkers too) *and* is full of Black and Brown staff
- Thinking and believing that "doing the work" is *only* about what white-led schools, school systems, networks, ed nonprofits, and education companies need to do and change
- Not being willing to examine and acknowledge nepotism, classism, elitism, colorism, ableism, homophobia, xenophobia, and more that can be alive and well within your school, network, district, nonprofit, or company even if it is led by a Black or Brown leader or predominantly Black or Brown staff team
- Being a nonprofit that centers nepotism (for their friends, fraternity brothers, sorority sisters, fellow alum of their alma mater or leadership programs, etc.) *and* is full of Black and Brown staff members

The list could go on and on.

Key Point

Don't assume your school, district, nonprofit, or company is sound and also equitable just because the leader, leadership team, or staff members are all or mostly Black or Brown.

If we go back to the story I began with of my blind spot of sexuality within the ice-breaker activity I led, you'll see that two things can be true at the very same time. Those two things are that I am a skilled DEI thought leader and facilitator, and at the same time, I have blind spots and things I have to still unlearn every single day. *As a* well-respected DEI facilitator and consultant, I still messed up by making that error and that showcases just how critical it is for all educators and educational leaders to engage in this work as an ongoing, never-ending process and journey.

So, let's first start with peeling back the layers of mindsets and beliefs that are truly necessary to even *enter* the conversation of advancing DEI work within schools.

Mindset 1: Diversity Is Deeper Than Just Race Alone

To engage in this work, you must decouple thoughts that DEI is exclusively about race. In fact, so often within the realm of education, and certainly outside of it, *diversity* is used as a synonym for *race*. In actuality, diversity is far deeper than race. Diversity is the variation of representation of any kind; it isn't therefore a synonym for discussion of race. Although racial diversity is *one type* of diversity, engagement in this work requires a lens shift to see diversity and DEI generally in its multiple forms. This means diversity also speaks to gender identity, religious background, socioeconomic or income/financial background, geographic origin, sexuality, language, neurodiversity, physical ability, and so much more. This means that as an educator, you must embrace a commitment to DEI as a commitment to examine the ways in which your school or district creates environments through policies and practices that positively develop and support the multiple identities our children hold—not just their racial identity alone.

In addition to their racial diversity, our students hold identities centered in their gender, neurodiversity, sexuality, physical and cognitive disabilities, language, socioeconomic status or background, religion, body size, personality types, and so much more. Not only is this the case for our students, though; it is also important to understand the range of diversity found among the adults within our educational leaders as well. Our staff members, employees, families, vendors, and other stakeholders hold difference within their own gender, neurodiversity, sexuality, physical and cognitive disabilities, language, socioeconomic status or background, digital literacy levels, educational attainment levels, personality types, and so much more.

Therefore, when we desire to focus exclusively on racial DEI, we must *state* and explicitly name it as such, so that the mere mention of DEI is not unspoken or coded language for support of children or adults of color or the tackling of racial matters within K–12 schools. When we mention DEI, we are committing to comprehensive work addressing the literal diverse identities our children and adults within our school communities hold. When we are exclusively focused on racial or race-based DEI work, we must call it that, and doing so shifts the thinking of communities to understand that what your school or district is addressing is the pursuit of racial equity and justice for those you serve.

Mindset 2: DEI Work Is for All Educators, Not Just White Ones

Have you ever heard someone say, "My school or district doesn't need DEI. Our staff is majority Black or Brown"? Have you yourself ever said or thought this? If so, you're not alone. For far too long, DEI work has focused on the work that white educators, particularly white educational leaders, need to do to create schools that Black and Brown children feel psychologically, emotionally, and physically safe within. Training and adult professional learning experiences of any kind aligned to this wave of thought automatically create thoughts and feelings of disconnect and disengagement for Black and Brown educators within those spaces. Over time, it can therefore create and reinforce a fixed mindset that DEI work isn't for Black and Brown educators, but rather exclusively for white people within the field. This then fails to enable the school and district to carefully examine and acknowledge the ways in which Black and Brown educators can perpetuate forms of harm, bias, and injustice on Black and Brown children as well as colleagues and other adults within school communities. It dangerously assumes that just because the educator is a person of color they have no unlearning and work to do because their mere racial or ethnic identity alone gives them a pass of being an automatically well-equipped person for the job of educating the hearts and minds of Black and Brown children. This could be the furthest thing from the truth.

One example would be a Black early childhood educator who has been socialized through a lens of colorism in their own upbringing that brings unconscious bias into a classroom in overly verbally affirming and always complimenting their students as being beautiful, gorgeous, handsome, or pretty who are of lighter complexion, those who are biracial, and those who are multiracial, but never verbally affirming or complimenting kids who are of darker complexion, more traditionally coarse hair textures, and so on, with those same adjectives or with any such affirmation.

The reality is that you do not have to be white to perpetuate colorism, classism, elitism, ableism, homophobia, xenophobia, and more. You simply have to be human. The reality is that educators of color are not immune to holding bias, prejudices, privilege, blind spots, and more. For example, a Black male educator can advocate that Black Lives Matter, and at the same time spew homophobic microaggressions to a Black male student in his care. Although it is far easier to celebrate a Black male educator in any school or district space because there are so few Black men within the profession of teaching, as educational leaders you must also be willing to sit with the cognitive dissonance and complexity of holding all educators responsible and accountable to doing right by children. By not addressing the harm that even a Black male educator can give to LGBTQ youth, you are sending a loud message that the only identity your school or district cares about is the racial or ethnic identity that students and staff members hold, but other aspects of who they are do not deserve protection, safety, love, and honor within your school or district.

Mindset 3: Effective DEI Work Requires More Than Training

Although providing professional development trainings for teachers, school support staff members, principals, central office staff members, superintendents, and other educators is important, it is not the only lever that drives this work. The reality is that we must undergo what Dr. Barbara J. Love coins as the development of a Liberatory Consciousness. In her framework of Liberatory Consciousness (Love, 2000), Dr. Barbara Love explains that there are essentially four phases of the continuum toward making any monumental change take place within an individual. In this case, I apply Dr. Barbara J. Love's framework to the process of undergoing change and sustaining change within schools and districts as a whole. Those four phases are: (1) awareness, (2) analysis, (3) action, and (4) accountability. Within the awareness phase, deep learning is key.

Schools and districts must first position themselves as learners in order to develop a clear understanding of what diversity is, what equity is and looks like, and what inclusion is and looks like. This includes learning the concepts, policies, and practices involved in order to build a vision for what the school or district can aim to become. For instance, there are many educators who profess to be equity advocates or DEI experts; however, if asked what equity is, they cannot clearly define the concept nor explain what it looks like in action. Although this is not a statement of attack to anyone, it is important to then ask the question of how an educator can champion, fight for, or advance something they can't even define. Therefore, it becomes very important for school communities and districts to first align on definition. What do we mean when we say *diversity*? How do we define this? What are we centering? Additionally, the question of inclusion follows suit. What is it? How do we define this as a school or district, and, most important, what does it look like in action? With a clear portrait of what the work is and what it is not, an educational leader is then equipped to begin a pathway of interrogation and exploration of where they and their school or district as a whole stand in relation to what they've learned.

Therefore, effective DEI work necessitates awareness building, which can come through training, small or large professional learning communities, and utilization of documentaries and film, lectures, literature, and other conduits for provision of knowledge. However, effective DEI work doesn't stop there with scheduling a DEI training and securing a vendor to lead it. Effective DEI work must transition from awareness building—which again can happen through training—to analysis or auditing of oneself, one's classroom, schools, and a district in its entirety. It is far easier to purchase culturally responsive pedagogy books for teachers and conduct professional DEI book clubs than it is to formally collect data via surveys, focus groups, interviews, and document/artifact review to understand and analyze the precise state of the school or district's areas of strength and areas for improvement as it relates to DEI for children and adults within the school or district as well. So, effective DEI moves from awareness building to analysis or auditing. This is followed by action. In other words, schools or districts must take their findings from analysis and auditing, and craft concrete plans of action and execute on those plans in order to ensure that money isn't simply invested in training but lacks follow-up and follow-through.

Operationalizing DEI within schools and districts requires the creation of action plans that denote what the school or district priorities are; what their goals and objectives are, or in other words, what they'd like to specifically achieve or accomplish in a specific area or aspect of DEI; what their strategies, activities, or actions will be to get there; who the owners are or who is responsible for what within their process of centering and executing what the school or district is endeavoring to do; and the timeline of when actions or steps will be taken. Last but not least, effective DEI work calls us to also be adamant in holding ourselves, our schools, and our districts accountable to visible and real change or growth. Once a school or district has created an action plan, they must, for instance, establish a time and space to regularly revisit their plan to monitor progress, adjust course, as well as celebrate wins and successes along the way. Even small wins and traction matters. Follow-up and follow-through is critical. The accountability aspect of a school's or district's DEI journey is also not something simply the principal, administrative or leadership team, or superintendent should exercise oversight over, but rather something schools and districts should invite varying members of their community to be able to exercise with and alongside them. Hiding your DEI plan through failing to be transparent with your stakeholders—be it teachers, parents, and students themselves, when it is developmentally appropriate to share, and others—doesn't equip them with the power to exercise community accountability, but only creates or deepens feelings of doubt, mistrust, and skepticism regarding the school's or district's stated commitment to this body of work.

Additional Mindsets

In addition to considering the previous three mindsets, the following mindsets and beliefs are important to embrace and keep at the forefront of your work as an educational leader. Each represents the original work and creation of nonprofit Dismantling Racism. Check out this excerpt from one of their latest publications (2016, p. 49):

- We need an analysis of how oppression and injustice works. This is not simply about reducing prejudice. This is about radically changing the way we do things.
- There is a difference between appreciating diversity and recognizing, being willing to acknowledge, and being willing to address oppression, injustice, and inequity wherever it exists.
- Building cross-cultural relationships is important.
- We have to be willing to do personal work, learn more about who we are, and change.
- We can't do this work alone or solo. We have to build a strong team of people committed to the same goal.

- We must be open to doing things differently, sometimes radically so, than we've done them in the past.
- We may have to redefine the very things we thought were basic.
- We need to learn that points of resistance, both within ourselves and as exhibited by others, are the sources of greatest learning.
- We must recognize discomfort as a signal for learning rather than an excuse for withdrawal or defensiveness.
- We need to acknowledge that we get out of this process what we put in. We must be open to learning even if it is not packaged in ways that we expect or in ways with which we feel comfortable. We must be actively engaged in the learning process.
- In this work, we must learn to seek to understand before turning to judgment. At the same time, we can expect—and we deserve—appropriate, loving, and just behavior.
- Change is often experienced by those in power as moving too quickly and by those with less power as moving too slowly. Change does not need to be slow, but often is.

All of these ways of thinking and operating help set the stage to advance racial equity both within your organization and in your work in partnership with external organizations.

WHAT ARE YOUR MOTIVES AND INTENTIONS?

As you begin your personal, departmental, school, district, or organization's DEI journey, there are a few preliminary questions I'd love to propose to you. If you are furthering or deepening your DEI journey, there are a few preliminary questions I'd love to propose to you as well.

For those who are new to this journey:

- What is driving your desire to begin this journey of building your awareness within the areas of DEI?
- What are your motives, intentions, hopes, and desires?
- Why do you feel or believe this is important?
- To what extent do your colleagues also feel and believe this body of work is important?
- To what extent does your manager, supervisor, or most senior leaders also feel and believe this body of work is important?
- Why does this matter to you? Why does it matter to your classroom, department, school, district, nonprofit organization, or education-related company?
- What benefits do you see this work having on the students you serve?
- What benefits do you see this work having on the families you serve?
- What benefits do you see this work having on the various community stakeholders you serve?
- Are you willing to engage in this work at the intrapersonal (inner work) level, which requires you to do your own private and internal work of reflection, acknowledgment, learning, unlearning, reconciling, healing, and growth?

- To what extent do you believe your colleagues are ready to engage in this body of work at the intrapersonal level (inner work)?
- Are you willing to engage in this work at the institutional level, which includes examining the values, beliefs, practices, and policies that govern your classroom, school, district, nonprofit organization, or education-related company's work?
- Do you believe your school, system, nonprofit, or organizational leaders are ready to engage in DEI work at the institutional level?

For those of you who are furthering and deepening the DEI journey you're already on:

- What was or has been your personal vision for DEI within your own personal and professional life? Is it clear and able to be articulated by others—those who champion this work with you as well as those you serve?
- What type of DEI have you been focused on driving within your classroom, department, school, district, nonprofit, or company?
- What are you most proud of within your current DEI journey?
- Where have you seen yourself progress the most in your learning and understanding?
- Has your focus been exclusive to one type of DEI agenda? If so, what type of diversity?
- If not, what are each of the types of DEI you have intentionally prioritized?
- What has your prioritization looked like and entailed (in practice not just theory)?
- What types or areas of DEI have you not considered, been as intentional about prioritizing and enacting, or hold as blind spots in your work?
- Of the types of diversity you have not considered, been as intentional about prioritizing and enacting, or held as blind spots in your work, which do you feel are most important to prioritize at this time?
- Which aspects of diversity has your school, district, nonprofit, or company not actively and explicitly centered to date?
- To what extent are you willing and ready to embrace the both/and dynamic of recognizing and embracing the expertise you hold within the arena of DEI, as well as being willing to admit where you still have room to grow?
- What do you believe will be most challenging?

Key Point
Your motives and intentions matter in this work. Performative DEI work stems from often superficial motives and questionable intentions. Ensure that you and your school or organization are committed to the journey in an authentic and honest way.

UNPACKING YOUR SOCIALIZATION

When I was in high school, I had the opportunity to apply and be admitted to a very highly selective, rigorous college preparatory public boarding school for the 11th and 12th grades. That experience changed my entire educational trajectory. Having attended "regular" public school from kindergarten to 10th grade, it also gave me a firsthand experience as to what inequities and disparities look like yet also what promising wealth lies within the same context of public schools. It was the first time I was in a racially diverse school setting. There were students who were Pakistani, Latino, Black, and white, living together in the sometimes very segregated and racially divided state of Alabama. Every teacher there was a college professor, so you had to have a doctorate to teach or a master's with so many years of collegiate teaching experience. I graduated from that institution and was afforded the opportunity to go to the University of Notre Dame. My peers had access to universities like Harvard, Yale, Spelman, Princeton, Emory, and more.

From that educational experience, I saw firsthand two wildly different spectrums of what education was like within my home state of Alabama. In one school, some of my textbooks—and this is in the early 1990s—were the same textbooks used in the 1970s. I opened them and could see people's names and when they used the book! There were the same water fountains that my parents had used at that school a generation earlier. When I went to boarding school, it was a whole other level. I took a marine biology class, and the school took us on a boat it owned to take us sailing on the Gulf of Mexico. While there, we captured squid to take back to our classroom to dissect. So in a lot of ways, I developed both an appreciation and a righteous feeling of anger that I had to leave my home and live three and a half hours away, at the age of 16, to have access to those advantages. And my peers whom I grew up with, who stayed at the local school, were on completely different life paths, not because they weren't capable or able or amazing and brilliant, but because they didn't have access to the same resources and opportunities. That fueled my commitment to fight educational inequities.

When I first started teaching, I originally came to Baton Rouge and taught in the Jackson-Clinton area. That later translated to me moving from teaching to instructional coaching in New Orleans, which led to principalship, which then evolved into educational consulting, which is what I'm doing now. And that was an intentional choice to say, "What are all the most beautiful experiences that I've had as an educator and what are the ugliest ones I've had, particularly as a Black woman in public education?" I began thinking about ways in which I could support and equip educators who looked like me—and even ones who didn't—with the skills, knowledge, and tools to create transformational spaces for kids. All this but not losing ourselves in the work or feeling that we have to assimilate and die inwardly, in order to be transformational.

I reflect often about best practices that I've enacted as a teacher and as a school leader, but I also think a lot about missteps and failures and errors on my part, as a teacher and as a school leader. If you're honest and transparent with yourself, and you lean into learning and growing, you can transform, and you can help people navigate those same waters. When I think about that scenario, I frequently consider how folks, as educators and even parents and community members, can be proactive, showing up on the front end for our young people, instead of the back end and being reactive, even with our policies. How are we fueling dollars and programs and putting supports in place to prevent things from happening?

Educational systems have a lot of power, in being able to help children see who they truly are and who they can be. In numerous ways, it shapes their schema of possibility. Conversely to that, when we're not intentional or when systems are not intentional, education systems have the potential to do the exact opposite. Sometimes they narrow and eliminate the focus and the vision of what children can be, what they can aspire to accomplish, and, in a lot of ways, crush the very essence of hope and optimism within them. Systems have the ability to foster liberatory thinking, particularly for Black and Brown children and other marginalized groups, because they can learn and discover ways of thinking, ways of resistance, ways in which communities—that our elders and ancestors who have come before us knew—have made sense out of. They have thought through community uplift and principles that foster the liberation of our entire community, not only in terms of financial freedom but also in the audacity to say to ourselves that no matter what we face, and no matter what we go through, we will overcome.

When systems are not intentional, they do the opposite in terms of fostering a means of thinking in which children believe that their story begins with slavery, an image in which we're the victim and not the victors. In which we passively experienced the oppression that we've had to experience face-to-face, without telling the story of the ways in which we have rejected that and fought and been resilient and have persevered. Educational systems have the ability to equip kids with technical knowledge, and also more qualitative and transformational knowledge, to be whoever they want to be. Conversely, when we're not creating high-quality educational environments, we cripple children's ability to live into who they actually want to be.

The things I've shared so far really speak to the children's experience of diversity, equity, and inclusion matters within schools and that is who we should be putting first in the conversation. Yet other folks experience our educational system: parents experience it, educators themselves experience it, and other stakeholders in education as well. I think a lot about preparation of teachers and preparation of educators, in general, even if they're principals, even if they're school social workers. The way in which we train and develop our practitioners matters. It's going to be harder for me as an educator to decipher and identify any issue if I don't have the lens to even know what the issue is and what the symptoms and/or manifestations of it could look like. There's room and space for our educators to be trained on not only what trauma-informed practices are but also the *why* and the *how*. What are the different types of trauma? What does it look like? And really, it helps adults navigate through their own traumatic experience because it's going to be hard for me to lead you to a place that I also haven't navigated. We need to create spaces for adults as practitioners to process their own experiences and how those experiences show up in the way they speak, the decisions they make, how they designed their classroom, and the rules and expectations they set for kids. We can provide space for a certain degree of healing for those adults. That, coupled with giving them the technical tools and the language and strategies and methods to really operate in a more trauma-informed way, is important because you have to balance the work of the head and the heart. You really are compelling a different way of thinking. You're shifting beliefs and you're shifting convictions, along with giving them actual tools. There's a delicate balance that comes through a series of professional development and adult learning opportunities.

When I think about being from Selma, and I think about civil rights history being a mandatory course that you're taking. I grew up knowing the names of giants so I didn't walk in my own city and not know the story of the soil that I was stepping on. So how do we say this is our city? For example, I am in New Orleans. What makes us New Orleans? How do we institutionalize that knowledge in schools? If our students are exposed to high traumatic experiences, how do we make sure that every educator in this system understands how to meet them where they are? There's something to be said about constantly asking questions. Where are we now? What's our community facing? How do we as a school system adapt to where we are at this moment? Because there's just not a permanent answer to that question.

Key Point

Welcome opportunities to reflect on how you've been socialized or conditioned.

The Role of Socialization

The mindsets covered previously in this chapter aren't exhaustive; there are many mindsets and beliefs that are important to embrace within this work, but I've found that for school leaders and educational leaders in general the main three we discussed are paramount within the current sociocultural and sociopolitical climate we live in.

- Diversity is deeper than race.
- DEI work is for all educators, not just white ones.
- Effective DEI work requires more than training.

If you can accept these mindsets, then you can also accept the fact that the additional inner work required to center and advance DEI will require your openness to revisit and examine how you were socialized as a child, young adult, professional, and more. *Socialization* is the process of conditioning a human being's thoughts, shaping a human being's beliefs, and teaching a human being how to act or behave.

Most individuals are socialized, for instance, to think of the color pink when they think of girls and the color blue when they think of boys, which is why it's no mystery that a great deal of gender reveal parties for expecting couples leverage those colors. Most individuals are also socialized or programmed to see, believe, and think certain things about people who are members of different groups, particularly racial and ethnic groups. What is programmed—depending on the group—may be positive things, negative things, or neutrality. Stereotypes are reinforced from generation to generation in this way, as well as narratives and perceptions of different groups. As you can imagine, socialization is informed by many different sources, for example, family members, such as parents, grandparents, or other caregivers; news media; books and magazines; K–12 schooling and higher education environments, particularly in curriculum; television and film; and more. An example of this may be bias and prejudice a person holds against a particular group based on how they were raised by their parents (e.g., the messages they shared with them about that particular group), what their K–12 school curriculum as well as teachers reinforced, and what was reinforced via archetypes portrayed through film, television, or via music.

In the words of Rev. Samuel Blakes, a popular New Orleans faith-based leader, "You cannot heal what you're not willing to reveal." When you are ready to truly center and advance DEI, you must be willing to unpack the messages you received, the ways you were taught to act and behave in relationships or interactions with different groups of people, and even the private thoughts that cross your mind about different groups of people that may be informed by media sources or even a lack of exposure to those groups or types of diverse identities.

In unpacking your own socialization, we must first own what the various thoughts and beliefs are that we currently have or have had in our past because denial of them gets us nowhere. Once we can take ownership, then it's key to also consider the sources that fuel our thoughts and beliefs because some centering and advancing DEI moving forward may mean that you lessen your engagement with certain sources that do not fuel accurate understandings of others. It may mean that you discontinue engagement with certain sources. It may mean that it will be important for you to diversify the sources of information that you intake so that you are able to deepen your understanding of others in a richer way.

It's not always easy to do this, especially when sometimes those skewed thoughts you have, the stereotypes that may be in your mind, or the beliefs you hold are informed by people you love, such as your parents, a close friend or mentor, your grandparents, or other loved ones. I was socialized, for instance, to believe that women are better seen than heard, which means that I was conditioned to believe that women shouldn't be outspoken. That was fueled not only by my grandmother, whom I absolutely love and adore, but by many in my church community growing up and even films and media I saw as a child and teen. Being socialized in this way translated into my adulthood, particularly within workplace environments, in my questioning myself and feeling imposter syndrome earlier on in my career when I wanted to speak and share within small- and large-group spaces. This means that I'd become afraid in the moment, I'd second-guess myself, or would simply feel as though what I wanted to share wasn't good enough or that I wasn't good enough to share, thus questioning my value. I have overcome that fear and insecurity over the years and am now very unafraid to publicly speak or express myself in any room or space that I find myself. However, I had to sit myself down and give myself space to reflect on where those fears and insecurities came from, and what fueled them, and then dive into the work of creating counter-narratives and counter-beliefs about myself and women in general.

Imagine still holding onto the beliefs I named and being in a role of educational leadership. Imagine the way that such beliefs could affect your practices and decisions within human resources (HR). It's possible therefore to be a woman in educational leadership who holds bias toward other women who are more vocal, outspoken, and advocate for themselves and others within a school. This means that as an educational leader—though you are a woman as well—you withhold promotions and opportunities for career advancement from those types of women. It means that you could or may also develop resentment or dislike for them that can translate into your performance evaluation of them, your day-to-day micro-interactions with them, and more. Though this is simply one example, the point is that unpacking your socialization has deep implications for helping you to begin to visit and identify how the not-so-good, skewed, inaccurate, and/or negative parts of your socialization shape how you show up today, your decisions, your inner or private thoughts, the things you say, and your actions as a leader, particularly when it comes to varying aspects and kinds of DEI.

If you are not willing to engage in the work of unpacking your socialization, it means that you are not willing to examine the reality that there are things in general that you have to unlearn and learn. It also means that you can bring a load of bias into your work every day as an educator that then gets experienced by your students, families you interact and engage with, and your very own colleagues. Microaggressions are a prime example of this. Microaggressions are the everyday verbal, nonverbal, and environmental slights, snubs, or insults, whether intentional or unintentional, that communicate hostile, derogatory, or negative messages to target persons based solely on their marginalized group membership (Diversity in the Classroom, UCLA Diversity & Faculty Development, 2014).

Imagine being a principal or teacher in a school of students who are racially diverse. Imagine being a principal of such a school that happens to include a growing number of students who identify as Asian American. Imagine how many educators hold assumptions—based on limited exposure within their own socialization—and assume that their Asian American students or their parents were born in a foreign country, not America. This could result in that principal or teacher saying things like "And where exactly are you and your family from?" or "You speak English very well. Your English is amazing!" Comments such as these assume the child and their family are not from the United States simply because of limited thinking and lack of exposure to information about the racial and ethnic diversity of our country, and also a lack of exposure in real life to Asian Americans. Without that exposure, people sometimes don't understand that a student or family of Asian descent, based on their physical appearance/features/attributes or self-identifying as such, doesn't equate to them being foreign born. That automatic leap of assumption—that if one looks different from the white norm, they must not be born in the United States of America— is traced thus to socialization in believing that being American born means you look a certain way or are of a certain race/ethnicity, which is not only limited but problematic because it's not accurate or true.

If you believe that you'd never participate in any of these racial examples and therefore you do not have the need to unpack your socialization, I have something for you to chew on. Imagine being an assistant or vice principal who was raised in the city that they are now leading within and growing up thinking that real and true success doesn't come from that place. In other words, say someone was raised to believe that in order to be successful, you must leave that town or city, and live and work elsewhere in order to make it in life. That belief and narrative holds power, and can filter into that assistant or vice principal's work with students each and every day, as well as their hiring practices within their school and their interactions with colleagues based on where those colleagues are from. It can translate into having or holding bias toward people who are from their own hometown (i.e., that city) in not hiring staff members for certain roles when you see that they were educated within that city's colleges or universities, believing that they have received an inferior education and believing that candidates whose degrees derive from institutions outside of that state hold more value and would bring more talent and worth to the campus. This bias rooted in that administrator's socialization can also translate to encouraging kids to think that they can only be successful if they choose to leave that locale/city/town.

As an educator within the city of New Orleans, Louisiana, I've seen the dynamics in these examples play themselves out within post–Hurricane Katrina educational practices, which is unjust to say the least. In the years immediately following the catastrophic natural disaster, many native New Orleanian educators had difficulty getting hired—after the historic mass firing of Black educators in the wake of that storm—because of stereotypes held about native New Orleanian educators being less competent, inferior, or not being good enough to educate our children as opposed to recent college graduates and educational leaders from other places within the United States, educators who were white and educators who were products of programs, such as Teach for America. This translated into résumés and applications not being reviewed and automatically being tossed out to interviews being denied to unnecessary interview steps being added to their process that weren't asked of other people.

Within some organizational settings, bias—particularly elitism, nepotism, and other forms of unfairness and injustice—can play out within the assumption and attribution of intelligence to certain candidates based on the type of four-year college or university they attended (e.g., overlooking candidates from historically Black colleges and universities, or HBCUs, versus those who are graduates from predominantly white institutions, or PWIs). Bias can also be attributed to the popularity of the teacher or leadership preparation program a candidate is a member or graduate of. This might look like showing preference for Teach for America corps members versus traditionally trained teachers within a public school system. I say that as a Teach for America alumnus myself watching this happen within contexts during the early 2000s at a time in which many Teach for America corps members were socialized within certain regions to believe that veteran educators within the profession were assumed to not add value and they as novice teachers were thus being brought in to "save the day."

The list of examples of the need to seriously examine what bias, mindsets, beliefs, schemas, stereotypes, and overall paradigms exist in your mind that can affect what you do every day and how you show up as an educator—be it a teacher, school leader, district leader, noninstructional staff member, nonprofit executive director of an education-support organization—can go on and on and on. The question isn't whether you hold any form of bias or whether you should unpack your own socialization. We all hold forms or types of bias even if it is subconscious. We all must examine both the beauty and joys of our socialization but also examine the problematic aspects and indoctrinations within our socialization as well. There are many things that influence our socialization. Some of those factors include but are not limited to our families, our peers, our schooling or educational environments, media, and more.

Key Point

Change begins with recognizing and admitting how you've been conditioned to see, think about, and even engage with varying groups of people. Until you're able to own your past and current socialization, you will always deny forms of bias and blind spots you may hold.

Questions to Ask Yourself

Here are a list of guiding questions I'd like to propose that you consider:

- What are the early messages you recall learning at home about other groups of people?
- Were they positive messages? If so, what were those messages and teachings? What specifically did you learn?
- Were they negative messages about any particular group of people? If so, what were those messages and teachings? What specifically did you learn?
- What messages have you internalized about a group based on what you've seen within television media, including movies, television shows, and films?
- What messages have you internalized about a group based on what you learned within a religious setting, such as a worship service, faith-based programming, and so on?
- What messages have you internalized about a group from your friends and social peers?
- What messages have you internalized about a group from your early childhood or K–12 schooling, especially teachings from curriculum and lessons or sayings from your teachers or educators within your grade school setting?
- What messages have you internalized about a group based on undergraduate or graduate school teachings?
- What messages have you internalized about a group based on professional membership organizations you're a part of?
- How do the messages you've considered from the previous reflection questions influence beliefs you hold today?

- How do these messages influence things you say as an educator, education practitioner, or educational leader?
- How do these messages influence actions you take and decisions you make for students?
- How do these messages influence actions you take and decisions you make for families?
- How do these messages influence actions you take and decisions you make for different sub-groups of staff?

This list of questions is not exhaustive, but it does push you to be mindful of the fact that you do in fact think things, believe things, speak things, and act on things you've learned or thoughts, mindsets, and beliefs you've developed about others—for good or bad. Your work on this journey of raising your awareness, and engaging in the lifelong walk of centering and advancing DEI is important. Next, you'll find a few key things I work to do every day:

- **Be mindful.** This is even in the most seemingly smallest moments, such as your daily or weekly morning dialogue with the mail delivery or postal service worker who delivers mail to your school all the way to the biggest moments of crafting policies that affect thousands of students and families within your school system.
- **Catch my thoughts. Take notice of my beliefs, mindsets, and the assumptions I am making.** As you know, denial gets us nowhere. No human is perfect nor holds perfection within the area of not possessing one ounce of bias, ignorance in an area of diversity, or transgression their entire lives—past and present. No one. It will always be important that you are honest with yourself about what transpires within your own mind. Catch the thoughts you have about students of color. Catch the thoughts you have about kids from lower socioeconomic backgrounds (i.e., students from low-income backgrounds). Catch the thoughts you have about single parents. The list goes on.
- **Self-correct.** Meet those thoughts that are problematic, biased, or seeded in any form of prejudice with counternarratives of truth. Combat stereotypes with a commitment to understand others, get to know others, and treat everyone—no matter who they are—with dignity, respect, and fairness. Meet your lack of knowledge in an area with curiosity. Ask questions. Dig and research to learn more about a group or type of person—in this case, students, families, colleagues, and other key stakeholders. Self-correct jumping to a conclusion about a family's value of education based on not seeing a parent, guardian, or caregiver at a parent-teacher conference or family engagement activities. Instead, meet that thought with curiosity to learn what may be the barrier to a parent's inability to attend the parent-teacher conference days your school hosts or the various family engagement initiatives your school hosts.

REFLECTION QUESTION

> **What are the micro things you do daily on your own walk to advance equity, inclusion, and diversity?**

UNLEARNING THROUGH CONTINUOUS LEARNING AND HEALING

"Everybody's journey is individual."

—James Baldwin

"Think of unlearning as a software update. Your devices need constant updates, so why wouldn't your knowledge?"

—Dom Murray

Many of us have been taught that it takes 21 days to build a habit, and sometimes, we even hear that it takes the same amount of time to break one. Although there is truth to that, for some acts, unlearning deep-seated messages, beliefs, stereotypes, and mindsets about members of a particular group requires more than a 21-day plan. Some of what goes unspoken is just how deeply infiltrated messages, beliefs, and mindsets about others or members of a particular group are. Some of what goes unspoken is just how many directions those messages have come from, which means that they have been compounded over time. That said, unlearning them isn't always easy in the sense that you cannot simply shake those thoughts away; however, anything takes root over time with repeated practice, new learning, and behavioral change. Unlearning entails the conscious and intentional choice to uproot and destruct anything that is no longer serving you, and, in this case, it is every form of oppression, harm, or prejudice that you can possibly think of. Just like any other habit that needs to be broken, unlearning in service to furthering DEI also requires the following.

Ongoing Learning

Be it through podcasts, online videos, books, articles, panels, formal and informal conversations with others, live or digital courses, and more, you must be committed to learning and consistently working to build and/or deepen your awareness.

Constant Self-Auditing

Amidst all that you are learning, it is really important to hold a mirror to yourself (and of course your institution as well, though we'll get into that more in the subsequent chapters of this book) against what you are learning to really conduct your own SWOT (strengths, weaknesses, opportunities, and threats) analysis of self. As you are continuing to learn, it's important that you do feel affirmation for the positive work you are doing (strengths) and are able to internally recognize and honor your wins and growth you're witnessing or experiencing within your own inner work, your words, and your actions, especially decisions you're making day-to-day. Auditing one self requires the ability to adopt a both/and mentality in knowing that although there are aspects of you that are intentional about DEI, conscious of your biases, well-meaning in your approaches, and even knowledgeable about aspects of DEI, you can still and do still have blind spots; you can still and do still make errors and perpetuate knowingly or unknowingly forms of injustice and/or inequity, and you can still learn more because no one can "master" all the many facets of DEI.

The Willingness to Own and Acknowledge Your Own Errors

As an educational leader, one of the best things you can ever do is display honesty, vulnerability, and transparency about your own growth areas within this work, weaknesses, and errors. What you model sets the tone for your campus, district, organization, or company. You will mess up. You will make mistakes. You will have things to unlearn, and pretending that you don't won't get you anywhere but rather contribute to the prohibition of a culture of vulnerability, self-reflection, and growth among those you lead and serve.

I think often about my early days of being an educational leader. I was an assistant principal and then became a school leader during what felt like the climax of educational reform, which was the early to mid-2000s. I can recall being socialized to believe that a *zero tolerance* and *no excuses* approach to student culture and discipline matters was the only way you could drive success. An example of my beliefs on discipline at that time were that our kids, who at the time were predominantly African American and from low-income or lower socioeconomic backgrounds, needed something more restrictive and nearly militant in approach to "keep them in line" or "in order" to ensure they were quiet, well behaved, and on task within our classroom learning environments. Within the last year of my principalship and the immediate years after I served as a school principal, I began to see how the approach of zero tolerance was unhealthy for children, paralleled a prison-like culture, and simply did not create the most optimal conditions for children to really just be kids. Although we facilitated fun activities for our children, such as popcorn parties, engaging field trips, surprise special guests, and so much more, in reflection I realized that my journey toward being a more equitable and inclusive leader would require me to unlearn the notion that maintaining great school culture and climate for our demographic of children meant that we also had to drive a zero tolerance approach (e.g., silent lunches as a behavioral consequence). You see, even as a strong Black woman educator, this mindset was one I embraced, not understanding that it was actually more harmful than it was helpful. Children living in poverty within urban and rural schools do not need a militant school culture and climate. Children of color within public and private schools do not deserve to be stripped of the opportunity to simply be kids and be provided robust opportunities for fun and joy. As I awakened to my own revelations through regrounding myself in literature of many different Black academic scholars in the education field, through exposure that came from opportunities to visit several different predominantly Black and also Title I schools (i.e., schools that are deemed federally as under-resourced and have higher populations of students receiving free and/or reduced lunch based on their families' socioeconomic status), I shed this notion and began to teach others, lead, and advocate within our field in a different way. My principalship began with the inheritance of what was considered a turnaround school or campus, which means that it was chronically academically underperforming and riddled with student discipline issues at the time of accepting the position. I was thus hired to help turn the school around, which meant I was hired to improve both the culture/climate of the school and its academic status. Because of the conditions of the school at that time, I believed that every single aspect of the school day needed to be scripted, managed, and controlled. I believed this—even as a Black woman educator—because of the challenging student behaviors—such as students hitting teachers, a high volume of out-of-school suspensions, and students running out of the school building—that needed to be directly addressed by my administration. I therefore operated with a zero tolerance mentality to ensure really tight or rigid student discipline policies and overall classroom management and student culture practices as a means of addressing a school culture that was previously chaotic and in ways unsafe, but most of all, also academically underperforming in its drop in the state's letter grade over time.

The practices I drove as a leader, our teachers drove within classrooms, and other administrators enacted helped us to dramatically reduce discipline problems within less than three months during my first year of school leadership. Out-of-school suspension went from nearly 55% (what it was the prior school year before I became principal and our administration took over) to under 5% within the first 6 months of my first year of principalship. The noticeable change in the environment being calm, quiet, and structured was incredibly salient not only to our staff members but also to members of our charter management organization's leadership team, to our students' families, and to observers and evaluators of education support organizations within my state.

Fast-forward to today, I can honestly say that there is so much I had to accept in recognizing the misalignment of my own values, hopes, and aspirations for youth, particularly those of color and those from low socioeconomic backgrounds, versus some of my practices as a leader. I had to unlearn the idea that compliance and order within a classroom was a sign of excellence for a failing school environment to recognizing that robust discourse (such as increased student voice and peer-to-peer engagement with a classroom) as well as physical movement (which is honestly the ability to let kids be kids, such as utility of dance breaks during the learning cycle and other means of making the learning experience fun) are not only okay but truly positive as key levers that could drive academic growth and high academic achievement within a failing school environment.

I had to unlearn the concept of zero tolerance for student culture and discipline and come to a place of understanding that it is possible to balance having clear standards and expectations for students (e.g., having a consequence ladder), but at the same time have a space that is developmentally appropriate, restorative, fun, and warm. I had to reckon with the fact that even as a Black woman in educational leadership, who herself had come from an impoverished socioeconomic background and was an avid advocate for Black and Brown children, I held problematic thinking that children from poorer financial backgrounds, who looked like me within a chronically failing school context, needed radically different (in relation to behavioral expectations) discipline practices and overall student culture. I was wrong. Doing better for me has meant the following:

- Being open and willing to learn about different student culture approaches and practices
- Being open and willing to reflect on and interrogate my own practices
- Being open and willing to take ownership for the amazing work and results of my leadership, as well as acknowledge and take ownership for practices within my leadership (as it relates to student culture) that in retrospect were problematic
- Championing better and more culturally responsive ways of driving student culture within chronically failing schools (often seen as "turnaround" schools)

Undergoing constant learning and unlearning has taught me how two things truly can be true at the same time. For me, those things were the realities of being a strong, effective, and culturally responsive educator (as a teacher and a school leader) and also enacting select practices that were not okay for the best and highest vision of what our children deserve.

Key Point
Never stop learning.

REFLECTION QUESTIONS

> **How often are you carving out intentional time for continuous learning? If so, what does continuous learning look like or entail for you?**

> **Are you willing to audit how you show up? Are you willing to audit the beliefs and mindsets you hold about others, particularly specific profiles of students, families, or even colleagues? Are you willing to interrogate your practices and decisions you've made in the past as a leader from a DEI lens?**

> **If the answer to the previous question is a *yes*, what do you feel will be the most challenging part of examining yourself or looking in the mirror?**

> **Whom can you learn from along your journey?**

Two

Operationalizing DEI Within Your School or District

To operationalize DEI within your school, district, nonprofit, or business, you must first be willing to undergo learning to build your awareness and understanding of what diversity is, what equity is, and what inclusion is. We cannot manifest, drive, or achieve something we cannot define or determine. If we proclaim that we advocate for equity, but cannot articulate what equity is nor what it looks like, how can we know that we have achieved it?

We must also organizationally and personally understand why DEI is important societally, within the education sector, and most important within your school community. In other words, our belief in the importance of this work and our authentic adoption of a DEI lens matters, and if we don't truly understand the significance of this body of work for our children, our teams, our families, and our communities, then we run the risk of engaging in the work in a half-hearted, performative, or superficial way.

In order to meaningfully center and operationalize this work, we must also be willing to surrender analysis of all aspects of our educational system instead of simply or only focusing our efforts on ensuring that classroom instruction is culturally relevant or responsive. A holistic approach to the work of centering and advancing DEI as a leader involves your willingness to analyze everything from your school board's governance to your budgeting processes to human resources (HR) within your school or organization to your interactions and engagement with your local community. Nothing is off limits to explore.

In order to support your journey to do so, this text is one tiny conduit for learning and development, but it is in no way exhaustive of the many different tools, resources, learning materials, and opportunities available to you, your leadership team, your staff members, and/or other key stakeholders—such as your school board members. As you engage on this journey, I highly recommend that you and your school community or organization get clear on what type of DEI you are seeking to drive and center within your work so that the learning opportunities you curate are aligned and not scattered or fuzzy for your team. This does not mean that you are ranking certain identity markers, lived experiences, backgrounds, or perspectives. It does mean that you are simply acknowledging that you cannot go deep on 59 different things at the same time but are making an intentional choice to dive deep in a segment of prioritized areas within your work so that you do not find yourself in a position of overpromising and under-delivering. You want clear focus so that your team is able to build a shared language, as well as a shared vision, of what DEI means, looks like in the area(s) of your focus, and how you will support your team as well as hold yourself and your team accountable in those areas.

The learning experiences you engage in as a school, school system, nonprofit, or company shouldn't be "one and done" opportunities either. In other words, they shouldn't be one-time engagements that enable you to check a box in saying that you've offered some form of DEI training for your team or that you yourself have "undergone" DEI training. A commitment to this work really is and should be an ongoing process of learning and, of course unlearning that occurs throughout the year, be it weekly, quarterly, monthly, longer deep dives multiple times per year, or whatever frequency works for your organization to provide really impactful, collective learning opportunities. Opportunities to learn also should be recurring as a symbol that DEI content and discourse is important and necessary for the work you do serving children, families, and communities every day. So, let's now dive into exploring the different components or domains of our work within the education field so that we know exactly where and how we should consider centering and advancing DEI!

Traditionally, conversations about DEI within schools have centered the actions teachers and school leaders should take in order to ensure that classroom instruction and classroom culture embrace the diversity of our students and ways to be as inclusive and equitable as much as possible. If you were to ask me how I championed DEI within the school I led as a principal years ago, the first response that would come to mind would be an explanation of how I led and guided our team to incorporate social justice education and other forms of culturally responsive teaching. As a former teacher and principal, I would have also answered that question in a purely racial way or a way that only centered the racial identity and diversity of the students I've taught or led over time. However, I submit to you that your journey toward centering and advancing DEI and our collective journey as a field should really extend far beyond just the classroom. There are a number of key areas that are essential to examine that extend beyond the classroom as the epicenter for DEI and extend far beyond the art and science of centering the racial identity of students. Moreover, there are a number of areas in which we should collectively deepen our learning beyond classroom practices and a conversation of race. Last but not least, there is so much you and we as a profession should audit and then begin to determine next steps that are deeper than the student experience and extend beyond race. Regardless of whether you are a teacher, literacy coach, assistant principal, school leader, superintendent, nonprofit leader, or education-adjacent business representative, it is thus essential for you to know and understand that inequity, harm, injustice, discrimination, and oppression within schools can and does takes place within all of these areas:

- Organizational clarity and commitment to DEI
- School board governance
- Organizational leadership and management
- Human resources (HR)
- Teaching and learning (instruction)
- Student culture and climate
- Operations and finance
- Family and community engagement
- Marketing, branding, and communications

We have to be willing to engage in deep thinking, conversation, and reform that addresses the need for DEI in all of these areas. When we imagine what it means to truly champion DEI within schools, we must imagine a comprehensive vision of all of these areas in order to ensure that both adults and students we serve can see, feel, and experience an appreciation for their diverse identities, a sense of belonging, and equitable practices and policies. Therefore, for each of the areas listed we need to learn to say the following:

- What does DEI mean in this area?
- What does DEI look like in this area?
- Is this an area of strength for me as a leader, our school, our district, or our organization as it pertains to how we center and advance DEI within this area? How do we know?
- Is this an area of weakness or challenge for us as it pertains to how we center and advance DEI as a school, district, nonprofit, or company in this area? How do we know?
- Is this an area that we've simply never considered or have not intentionally or deeply held as an area we need to center and advance DEI within?

In this part of the book, you'll find the following:

- A general framing of the relevance of each of the aforementioned areas of school operation as opportunities to operationalize DEI within
- Guiding questions for formal and informal analysis and auditing purposes
- Relevant existing frameworks that provide ideas and ways to enact DEI within each area
- Sample action items or next steps you could take within each area of focus
- A relevant story or case study that will help you further internalize the significance and need for an intentional DEI lens within each area

Key Point
Centering DEI should extend far beyond classroom-based efforts. Every domain of operation within a school represents an opportunity to engage in DEI analysis and intentionally center and advance it within the field of education. The refusal to examine the ways in which inequity and harm are perpetuated outside of the classroom gives further permission for said realities to grow.

CHAPTER 3

Organizational Clarity and Commitment

This area is perhaps the most foundational place to start your DEI journey as an educator or educational leader. Organizational clarity and commitment speaks to whether you, your team, or your organization have clearly defined the role of DEI within your work and within your organization as a whole, as well as what these concepts mean for you as an institution. Organizational clarity and commitment speaks to whether you have made a formal (not just informal, casual, or unspoken) commitment to DEI, and, to the extent that you have, where it lives even in writing or formal written language, how it is communicated, and how it is actually enacted with your stakeholders: staff members, students, families, peer institutions in the work, or anyone for that matter. When organizational clarity is present within a school, district, nonprofit, or company as it relates to DEI, the organization and all employed by it can clearly define what diversity means for them as an institution, what inclusion means and looks like within their organization, and what equity is and looks like within your organizational work. If you work for an organization that has made some type of formal commitment to center and advance DEI but staff members and other stakeholders within your work aren't even on the same page about what these terms mean, that's not a good sign but rather a flag that organizational clarity as it pertains to DEI may not be present. If I were to pull a random member of your team and ask them what does *equity* mean and how does your district drive equity, could they clearly define this concept and how it shows up in action within your district? Or, would people have different interpretations of this word or be unsure altogether? Would they be able to articulate how your district drives equity (e.g., the strategies of how you do it and what your DEI-oriented goals are)? Those are very real questions that speak to whether it is truly embedded or not within your organization, whether folks understand it or not, whether it lives and breathes in action or not, and whether a few people or a singular person is the holder of your DEI work versus the collective body or team being actively engaged in the work.

Overall, this first domain—organizational clarity and commitment—is composed of the following:

- Clarity of your school, network, district, nonprofit, or company's *why*
- In other words, what compelled you to kickstart your DEI journey or what are the origins essentially of your DEI work

- The development of shared language
- Development of your DEI vision or clarity as to what your DEI commitment is
- How you internally and externally communicate your DEI commitment
- How you invest and engage various stakeholders in your DEI commitment and work
- The development of a DEI plan
- Progress monitoring and evaluation of your DEI plan

Because I've noted what organizational clarity entails, know that the second bulleted item is critically vital because it is the springboard for ensuring that you and your team are actually normed and agree on what diversity is, what inclusion is, and what equity is and is not. If you do not, you risk having your team operate within a very narrow focus of what diversity actually is and therefore miss opportunities to operate with increased depth and intentionality as it pertains to the intersecting identities our students hold as well as our staff members, families, and community stakeholders. This means that we may not be intentional when it comes to our mindfulness in practices, policies, and infrastructure of gender identity, neurodiversity, sexuality, socioeconomic background, body image, and more.

If you do not build a shared language, you also risk the utility of these terms as simply buzzwords within your school, district, nonprofit, or company. This is especially true for the word *equity* because at this time it is easily tossed around within our national education ecosystem. So, taking the time to clearly define DEI and to create a clear and compelling vision of what it will look like in action educating children, leading adults, and operating a system or institution in general is essential.

Once you've done so, it will be important to determine how, when, and where you will communicate your commitment internally with your own team and how, when, and where you will do so for your external audience, which are families, vendors, key community stakeholders, and more. No one will have to guess where you stand when it comes to DEI when you are clear in your message and thoughtful about where and how you will communicate it. Last but not least, when it comes to investing and engaging your team in DEI work, you will need to determine what your strategies are for centering DEI, what actions you and others on your team will take, what your goals or desired outcomes are, who will own what, timing, and what resources engaging in this work will require. In essence, you need a plan and you will need to monitor execution of your DEI plan over time to ensure that you truly are walking out what you are talking, making adjustments over time where needed, and also honoring your progress.

CASE STUDY: ISIDORE NEWMAN

As an example, I want to first show you how the board of directors for a private Pre-K–12 school created a shared language of these terms not only for themselves but for all of their four school campuses. The school is Isidore Newman School. Located in the heart of uptown New Orleans, Newman is the only NAIS-accredited, coeducational, nonsectarian, independent day school in the city of New Orleans. One of the places its formal written DEI commitment lives is on their school's website—for instance—to provide open access to anyone who wants to see it and learn about their journey of commitment moving forward to DEI. Here is how the Newman board of governors define the concepts themselves:

> *Consistent with ISAS standards, the Board of Governors seeks to ensure that Newman fosters an environment of Diversity, Equity, and Inclusion at school and among the Newman community. Our School continues to be unequivocal in actively opposing racism in all forms. An important aspect of the Newman experience is based on building relationships across a diverse group of people. These relationships provide the trust to engage in difficult and complex conversations and lead to a better understanding of different perspectives and allow us to embrace the humanity in one another.*

Definitions:

> *Diversity is defined as the wide range of characteristics that contribute to a person's identity including, but not limited to, ethnicity, race, gender, religion, age, ability, sexual orientation, and socio-economic background.*
>
> *Equity is defined as fair treatment and processes that ensure equal access to opportunity. As a function of fairness, equity ensures that people have what they need to participate in school life and realize their potential.*
>
> *Inclusion is defined as belonging and means that each student feels accepted, empowered, and affirmed.*

So, let's dissect this.

REFLECTION QUESTIONS

What is the power of the board of the school setting this tone for their school community? What are the implications of this work being led by the board of governors on the overall institution's pathway moving forward?

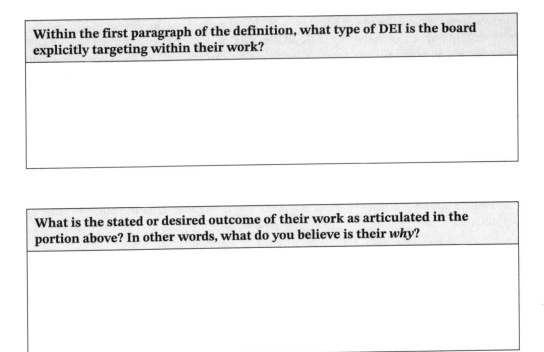

Within the first paragraph of the definition, what type of DEI is the board explicitly targeting within their work?

What is the stated or desired outcome of their work as articulated in the portion above? In other words, what do you believe is their *why*?

There are tremendous benefits for educational institutions being on the same page about terminology and their vision for their work. The ideal scenario within our profession would be having board members, school leadership team members, central office staff members and leaders, all school-based staff members (instructional and noninstructional), families, students (in a developmentally appropriate way), and other stakeholders such as its vendors being on the *same* page about and also invested in or bought into the institution's commitment to this work.

However, in real life, this is rarely the case. Sometimes, you have a board that is highly committed to the work, but the organizational leaders—such as the CEO of a charter school network or a superintendent of a traditional school district or the head of school for a private school, for instance—are not. Sometimes, you have organizational leaders of a school, system, or network committed to the work but their board is not. There are many different scenarios that play out for good and bad in that the work gets stifled, roadblocked, or lacks sustainability over time, which prevents it from being able to meaningfully take root in implementation throughout classrooms, operations, finance, governance, and all other aspects of a space.

Beyond shared language and understanding of terms, having a shared vision is about establishing clarity as to what your commitment to DEI is or will be. This prevents anyone from having to guess what your commitment is or whether you have one. Your commitment should drive your development of a concrete plan, which means that it should drive your actions and strategy. Now, let's take a look at Isidore Newman's commitment to diversity as stated on its website:

> *Our Position on Diversity:*
>
> *The Board firmly embraces and strongly advocates diversity at Newman in the student body, school leadership, faculty, staff, and board. The Board believes diversity is an important component of a Newman education, exposing students to diverse viewpoints and experiences. Diversity benefits the entire community and prepares graduates to thrive in a global economy and a diverse world. The Board believes that a diverse faculty and administration bring varied life experiences and viewpoints beneficial to all students and enriches the Newman community. Students should see themselves represented in all levels of the Newman faculty, administration, and staff. The pace of increasing diversity will be guided by the qualitative judgment of the Board and the administration with continued input from the Newman community. The goal is to increase diversity across all constituencies in ways that are consistent with the school's mission and high standards. The school administration will report regularly to the Board on its efforts and progress in increasing diversity.*

REFLECTION QUESTIONS

What do you notice in the statement of commitment to diversity? What is most pronounced?

What does your own commitment to diversity entail?

Here are a few things that stand out to me:

- Newman's diversity statement clearly shares with Newman's audiences what the institution's application of a diversity lens actually applies to. It explicitly calls out the fact that creating a diverse body applies to the composition of its student body, school leadership, and faculty, staff, and board members.
- This diversity statement explicitly calls out what the board of governors feel is the return on investment or benefits of diversity for their institution, which essentially helps an institution understand its *why*.
- This diversity statement explicitly states that there is not a clear "pace of increasing diversity," and that the increase of diversity "will be guided by the qualitative judgment of the Board and the administration with continued input from the Newman community." This also opens the door for a number of possibilities for different stakeholders (staff members, parents/families, donors, etc.) to ponder:
  - What led to an explicit stance to not have quantitative targets, quotas, or goals in this area?
  - What is at stake by not having quantitative targets, quotas, or goals in this area?
  - What is gained by not having quantitative targets, quotas, or goals in this area?
  - Who sets the tone for knowing what enough (in terms of diverse representation) is or looks like if there are no explicit aims the organization is driving toward?
  - What will the process of stepping back and assessing progress entail?
- This diversity statement explicitly shares what one form of accountability will be for their progress in this area.

The purpose of sharing this statement isn't to say that it is exemplary nor to say that it is a poor deliverable, but rather to lift one example for your review so that you can see exactly what I mean when I say that you have to be clear about what these concepts are, what they mean to your institution, and what role they play within your work.

Building on this school community's diversity segment, next you'll find the excerpt of Isidore Newman's commitment to equity specifically:

Position on Equity:

All students should have equal access to the opportunities and resources at Newman School. Given that students and families have a range of access to resources, both financial and otherwise, Newman will strive to provide compensating school-related resources to the extent possible.

All students are held to the high expectations and challenges of a Newman education.

Newman strives to provide individualized social and emotional support that addresses the diverse range of student experiences and needs. It is important for students and their families to be made aware of resources that are available to them, and how to access them.

Newman has high expectations for student behavior. Teachers and school administrators will address mistakes and behavior inconsistent with school policy in an equitable and consistent manner to ensure that all students are treated fairly.

REFLECTION QUESTIONS

What do you notice in the previous statement of commitment to equity? What is most pronounced?

What does your own commitment to equity entail?

Now let's look at the school's position on inclusion:

Position on Inclusion:

Newman values each individual. Our goal is for each individual to have a strong sense of belonging. All members of the Newman community should feel included, appreciated, seen, known, and heard.

Newman should have an inclusive, balanced curriculum that provides a diversity of voices and viewpoints to reflect the history, experiences, and cultures of all people. The curriculum should be broad-based, recognizing the different perspectives that students bring to intellectual inquiry and engagement.

All members of the community adhere to the Newman Principles for Civil Discourse in expressing and discussing ideas and perspectives, while recognizing that behavior that violates our policies against violence, discrimination, harassment, and hate is not acceptable. We encourage curiosity and open mindedness in engaging with ideas that are different from our own.

Newman strives to create a more inclusive, civil, and unifying environment so that acceptance and support of all students and members of the community, no matter their differences, is a natural extension of school culture.

REFLECTION QUESTIONS

What do you notice in the statement of commitment to inclusion? What is most pronounced?

What does your own commitment to inclusion entail?

CASE STUDY: LYNBROOK

Now, let's explore the DEI commitment, the vision, and the strategies of a different school system that is publicly posted online. This example centers the work of Lynbrook Public Schools, which is found within Lynbrook, New York. The following information is found on their district's website page.

Overview

Lynbrook UFSD is committed to supporting diversity, equity, and inclusion (DEI). In each school, a Diversity Committee has been established to discuss building-based efforts and concerns regarding DEI. In addition to the building committee, the students in Lynbrook High School have also established a Student Diversity Committee as well. Members of the building-based committee, including students, parents, teachers, and administrators, come together to form the District Diversity Council. The District Diversity Council meets every other month to share ideas and help unify efforts to meet the goals stated in the District's DEI Plan.

District Diversity Council Mission Statement

The mission of the Lynbrook Diversity Council is to support the school district in finding resources which will assist in building professional capacity, increasing and enhancing community connections and involvement in our schools, elevating student voices in our processes, and working together to create environments that will enhance each student's self-esteem, promote discovery of and maximize individual student potential, and guide each to dignify, appreciate, respect, accept, and value human diversity.

District Diversity Council Belief Statements

Each student will learn in an environment that promotes diversity, equity, and inclusion.

Each student will seek to understand the complex and rich identities of self and others.

District Equity Plan Priority Areas

1. *Developing inclusive curriculum, instruction, and assessment K–12.*
2. *Strengthening and creating opportunities, access, and educational quality for all students in our diverse community.*
3. *Prioritizing student input to develop practices with a more equitable framework.*
4. *Promoting intentional hiring practices that encourage candidates from diverse backgrounds to apply for open positions.*

Priority Area #1: Developing inclusive curriculum, instruction, and assessment K–12.

Goals

1. *Provide K–12 curricula and assessments that focus on diversity, equity, inclusivity, and cultural responsiveness.*
2. *Foster culturally responsive pedagogy and inclusive practices that affirm and support the diverse identities and experiences of our students.*
3. *Improve the use of student voice in developing curriculum material and educational experiences.*

Objectives

1. *During the 2021–2022 school year, all schools should have a constant faculty agenda item dedicated to the Culturally Responsive-Sustaining Education (CRSE) Framework.*
2. *During the 2021–2022 school year, offer all teachers professional development on topics such as managing difficult conversations, culturally responsive pedagogy and inclusive practices that affirm and support the diverse identities and experiences of our students, et cetera.*
3. *By October 2021, each secondary building diversity committee should elect two student leaders to serve as contributing members of the District Diversity Council.*
4. *By the end of the 2021–2022 school year, all school building diversity committees, composed of staff, students, and parents, will meet at least quarterly to discuss diversity, equity, inclusivity, and cultural responsiveness and the development of homework, assessment and grading practices that support diverse needs.*
5. *By the end of the 2022–2023 school year, generate lists of student literature explicitly taught and available as choices at each grade level and note the inclusivity of authors from diverse backgrounds and perspectives.*
6. *By the end of the 2022–2023 school year, generate lists of monthly lessons taught in each building by grade level that include aspects of empathy, tolerance, diverse perspectives, and civic responsibility.*
7. *By the end of the 2023–2024 school year, establish positions for "Lynbrook Culturally Responsive Education Leaders" (LCREL) for each school building to support other educators who are in the process of implementing strong culturally responsive and equity strategies within their classrooms.*

Priority Area #2: Strengthening and creating opportunities, access, and educational quality for all students in our diverse community.

Goals/Action Steps

1. *Promote a sense of belonging and an inclusive learning environment through instructional approaches, curriculum taught and assessed, and events celebrated.*
2. *Identify and address any inequities and/or opportunity gaps, if any, that exist in the areas of academics, discipline, and attendance.*

Indicators to Track Priority Area #2

1. *Continue to utilize the building level diversity committees and district-wide Diversity Council to examine instructional approaches, curriculum taught and assessed, and events celebrated.*

2. *Continue to support annual sensitivity workshops for students and families K–12 scheduled age appropriately (e.g., promote anti-bullying and up-standing, celebrate differently abled students, foster culturally responsive communities, embrace racial and ethnic differences, promote LGBTQ+ rights and sexual harassment awareness, etc.).*

3. *Continue to work with families with diverse needs and provide services to meet those needs. This can include offering classes focused on supporting students.*

4. *During the 2021–2022 school year, start collecting and reviewing various forms of data and analyze any inequities and/or opportunity gaps.*

5. *During the 2022–2023 school year, work on proactively identifying learning deficits early in students' educational careers to alter their academic trajectories by revisiting kindergarten screeners.*

6. *During the 2022–2023 and 2023–2024 school years, monitor identified academic and perceived opportunity gaps for student success and begin to implement student specific supports, such as mentoring, additional support classes, and tutoring.*

7. *During the 2022–23 and 2023–2024 school years, explore further use of standards-based grading (K-8).*

Priority Area #3: Prioritizing student input to develop practices with a more equitable framework and offer shared cultural experiences.

Goals/Action Steps

1. *Introduce or redesign courses of study that students feel are relevant for their educational experiences.*

2. *Reflect the diversity of our school community in the programs, experiences, and opportunities that are offered.*

Indicators to Track Priority Area #3

1. *During the 2021–2022 school year, survey high school students to ascertain areas of interest and gather supporting information for curriculum strands.*

2. *During the 2022–2023 school year and beyond, organize an annual high school student-led community forum that brings our diverse community together to discuss issues and topics related to equity.*

3. *During the 2022–2023 school year, all building level diversity committees will review and discuss, with the input from students, the diverse perspectives in the literature studied and the national cultural months and holidays celebrated and report their findings to the district-wide Diversity Council.*

Priority Area #4: Help create intentional hiring practices that encourage candidates from diverse backgrounds to apply for open positions.

Goals/Action Steps

1. *Attempt to diversify the professional staff so students see themselves reflected in their educational role models.*

Indicators to Track Priority Area #4

1. *During the 2021–2022 school year, work with local colleges and universities to create an outreach network that encourages students from diverse backgrounds to participate in our application processes.*
2. *During the 2021–2022 school year and beyond, further develop partnerships with higher education programs specifically focusing on helping to prepare teacher candidates from diverse backgrounds.*
3. *Upon adoption of the plan, include the District's diversity statement on postings for available positions in the district.*

REFLECTION QUESTIONS

What is the power of a DEI working group—in this case an assembly of diversity councils—setting the tone for their school district's DEI work? What are the implications of this work being led by a DEI working group on the overall institution's pathway moving forward?

What do you notice in the organizational commitment excerpt from this particular public school district? What is most pronounced?

SAMPLE FRAMEWORKS

As an educational leader, your development of shared language and a clear DEI vision should be grounded in some form of research and/or evidence-based framework, the lived experiences of marginalized communities and voices, the scholarship of members of marginalized communities and organizations led by marginalized communities, and those who are most directly and disproportionately affected by the inequities and injustices we should be fighting to address.

One example of a framework that centers race exclusively was created by Crossroads Ministry in Chicago, Illinois, adapted from its original concept by Bailey Jackson and Rita Hardiman, further developed by Andrea Avazian and Ronice Branding, and then further adapted by Melia LaCour, Puget Sound Educational Service District. This framework, called "A Continuum on Becoming an Anti-Racist Multicultural Organization" is a racial DEI framework in particular. It focuses on adults' experiences within organizations, so as an education leader and from a racialized lens, review it in thought of your teachers, noninstructional staff members, middle leaders, assistant principals, principals, network and/or district leaders, nonprofit colleagues, board of directors, and business colleagues.

Next, you'll find an example of a different framework that centers multiple forms of student identity beyond race alone and how teachers can be culturally responsive in their approach and lens to the work. It draws on the research and scholarship of greats such as Dr. Gloria Ladson Billings, Dr. Geneva Gay, and many more legends within this body of work, and was created by the Region X Equity Assistance Center at Education Northwest.

CASE STUDY: REGION X EQUITY ASSISTANCE CENTER AT EDUCATION NORTHWEST

In 2016, the Region X Equity Assistance Center at Education Northwest released the following framework for schools to support teachers in creating an equitable classroom environment:

> *Teachers must be intentional about eliminating bias and creating a culturally responsive classroom climate. Each of us has biases that influence how we talk and relate to students and colleagues. Research suggests six strategies that teachers should implement to create an environment in which all children have equitable opportunities to learn (Morrison, Robbins, & Rose, 2008; New York University, 2008).*

Teachers acknowledge their own biases and inequitable actions when they:

- *Participate in professional development on harassment and equity issues.*
- *Treat others with respect regardless of their race, national origin, sex, or disability.*
- *Improve their communication skills by listening and adjusting to the communication style of others, continually checking for understanding, respecting differences, and using language that builds trust and positive relationships.*

- *Remember that differences in communication style can lead to misunderstandings. In some cultures, a "thumb's up" sign means everything is okay, but in others it is a rude sexual sign.*
- *Are honest if they are unfamiliar with another culture.*
- *Pay attention to how others respond to what they do and say. Ask if there are times when others may view their behavior as disrespectful or harassing.*
- *Do not assume that others enjoy comments about their appearance, hearing sexually or racially oriented jokes, or welcome being touched without their permission. Remember that students may not tell them if they are offended or feel harassed by what they say or do.*

Teachers make an effort to learn about their students' cultural backgrounds when they:

- *Plan classroom activities that help students learn more about their cultural backgrounds.*
- *Include activities such as family history projects, selecting readings about the cultures of students in their classroom.*
- *Ask families or community members for information about the cultural background of students.*
- *Plan family nights or cultural events that encourage discussion and learning about others in their school.*

Teachers examine curriculum and learning materials for bias when they ask:

- *Does the curriculum provide for a balanced study of world cultures?*
- *Does the curriculum teach students about the contributions of men and women from different cultural backgrounds? Do classroom learning activities promote appreciation for non-European cultures?*
- *Does the curriculum include information about the past and present experiences of people from different cultural backgrounds? Of both women and men?*
- *Are issues and perspectives of minority groups included?*
- *Do textbooks and course materials avoid sexual, racial, and cultural stereotypes?*
- *Are opportunities to explore the perspectives of individuals from different backgrounds included?*
- *If the curriculum contains biased information or stereotypes, is this pointed out and are students provided with more accurate information?*
- *Do classroom displays and instructional materials include positive representations of diverse international and domestic cultures?*

Teachers build caring, cooperative classroom environments when they:

- *Immediately confront any biased or discriminatory behavior in the classroom or school.*
- *Create a safe, comfortable classroom environment in which students feel comfortable talking about harassment.*
- *Teach students how to treat each other with respect.*

Teachers build relationships with families and communities when they:

- *Create a representative team of school administrators, teachers, school counselors, parents, and students to guide and implement approaches to prevent harassment.*
- *Build partnerships with community members, youth organizations, and other service providers.*
- *Invite local community groups to make presentations and conduct workshops for teachers and students.*
- *Create and distribute a directory of diverse local consultants throughout the district.*
- *Develop strong linkages with families and community members. For example, producing a handbook for parents may help reduce concern for their child and build support for your school's harassment prevention program.*

Teachers identify curricular bias by looking for these practices:

- *Invisibility—Overlooking certain groups that implies they are less valuable or important.*
- *Stereotyping—Limiting the opportunities for a certain group based on rigid perceptions of their ability or potential.*
- *Imbalance or selectivity—Providing one viewpoint or selective information that leads to misinterpretation or an incomplete understanding of an event, situation, or group of people.*
- *Fragmentation or isolation—Placing information about people of color, women, or other protected groups in a box or chapter that is separate from the main body of text.*
- *Linguistic bias—Using masculine words such as* he *and* mankind *exclusively, or using patronizing terms such as* needy *or* less fortunate *to describe a group of people.*

REFLECTION QUESTIONS

What do you notice in the sample framework? What is most pronounced?

If you, your school, your system, your nonprofit, or organization of any type already use a specific framework, what do you love the most about your existing framework? Conversely, what is it missing or does it need to further address?

FINDING A FRAMEWORK YOU CAN LEVERAGE

I encourage you to find a framework, theory, and/or body of work that defines what DEI look like in action. Find one that speaks to and resonates with what you are trying to achieve as an organization. How can you strive toward what you do not know, have not seen, or cannot conceptualize? Why guess when you can rely on clear and concrete tools, resources, and artifacts that can help you along your journey?

As you contemplate theories, models, frameworks, tools, and resources to leverage, I'd encourage you to pay attention to the following:

The Source
- Who is the author or people who have created or produced this?
- Is this person credible? If so, how do you know?
- If not an individual person, what organization produced this?
- Is this a credible organization? If so, how do you know?

      When I say credible, I'm not necessarily speaking to how many awards or accolades they've won as opposed to their level of subject matter expertise, their receipts, or, in other words, the evidence of their effectiveness or track record of success, from doing or being directly engaged in this body of work, and/or their lived experience being incredibly proximate to or directly affected by the work/topic area. In relationship to organizations, I'm not necessarily speaking to how many awards or accolades the organization has won, as well as how popular, large, or well-known, as opposed to the organization's overall level of subject matter expertise (i.e., who are the subject matter experts within the organization itself), the organization's overall receipts from doing or being directly engaged in this body of work, and/or the organization's proximity to or its degree of being directly affected by the work/topic area as an organization.

The Focus
- What does this tool drive and center?
- Does it center a particular type of identity or is it intersectional in nature?
- Does it center diversity?
- Does it center equity?
- Does it center inclusion?
- Does it center another concept that is related and yet also important (such as justice)?
- Does this tool's focus align with the current focus we want to drive and center within this moment of our DEI journey?

The Substance
- Does the content make sense? Do you understand it?
- Is the content coherent?
- Does this framework, tool, or resource establish a clear trajectory, continuum, or schema for me (as a leader), our school, our nonprofit, or our company to use to imagine and draft our own vision, goals, and/or strategies for centering and advancing DEI?

With these questions in mind, I'm sure you'll find what works best for you. Every education nonprofit is different. Every education company is different. Every school community and district is different. Given your unique context and the conditions in which you are doing or will engage in this work, you must utilize that information to make an informed decision of a tool, resource, or framework that will or can ground your work.

GUIDING QUESTIONS

Now that you've seen examples and heard the context of why starting with examination of your organization's overall clarity and commitment to DEI is a foundational or fundamental part of your organization's DEI journey, let's look at what central or guiding questions your organization should be asking yourselves formally or informally to guide your ability to truly get clear on what DEI means to you and what role it will play within your work. I propose that you ask yourselves these questions:

- Does your organization understand why it's important to prioritize diversity?
- Does your organization understand why it's important to prioritize inclusion?
- Does your organization understand why it's important to prioritize equity?
- Has your school, district, network, nonprofit, or company made a formal institutional commitment to addressing inequity and injustice?
- Has your school, district, network, nonprofit, or company made a formal institutional commitment to centering and advancing DEI?
- Does your organization explicitly name your commitment to advancing DEI in internal policies, practices, and external messaging/communications?
- Does your school, district, network, nonprofit, or company understand that centering and advancing DEI extends beyond teaching and learning, but can encompass multiple aspects of your organization's operation(s)?
- What informed the commitment of your school, district, network, nonprofit, or company, and who made it?
- How does your school, district, network, nonprofit, or company embed or connect DEI to your mission, vision, core values, and/or theory of change?
- To what extent do you feel that teachers and noninstructional staff members are invested in your vision and commitment to DEI? How do you know?
- To what extent do you feel that school leaders and other school-based middle leaders are invested in your vision and commitment to DEI? How do you know?
- To what extent do you feel that central office staff members/leaders, as well as the senior executive leaders of your organization, are invested in your vision and commitment to DEI? How do you know?
- To what extent do you feel that parents, families, and guardians are invested in your vision and commitment to DEI? How do you know?
- To what extent do you feel that board members (elected or appointed)—depending on the type of institution you are—are invested in your vision and commitment to DEI? How do you know?
- What are the short- and long-term benefits of your commitment to DEI?
- Does your school, district, network, nonprofit, or company use a specific DEI toolkit to analyze and review your policies, practices, procedures, and data (both qualitative and quantitative) on a regular basis (including, but not limited to, budgeting, programmatic efforts, communications, recruitment and hiring, human resources, development, etc.)?
- Does your organization have a written DEI plan with clear actions, timelines, people responsible for each action, indicators of progress, and processes for monitoring and evaluation?
- If you have developed or are developing a written DEI policy and/or plan, were representatives or are representatives from marginalized communities participants in its development?
- If you have developed or are developing a written DEI policy and/or plan, were representatives or are representatives of your student body (if it is age or developmentally appropriate) involved in its development?

- If you have developed or are developing a written DEI policy and/or plan, were representatives or are representatives from your students' family, parent, and/or guardian base participants in its development?
- If you have developed or are developing a written DEI policy and/or plan, were representatives or are representatives from your staff members participants in its development?
- If you have developed or are developing a written DEI policy and/or plan, were representatives or are representatives from any other key roles within your school, nonprofit, or company participants in its development?
- Does your organization have clear and/or explicit key performance indicators that define what matters most to you in your journey of centering and advancing DEI?
- Does your organization have clear and/or explicit goals and milestones to track your progress toward centering and advancing DEI?
- How will your organization measure your DEI goals and milestones?
- Are your strategies toward driving DEI aligned to your DEI vision? If so, how do you know?

REFLECTION QUESTIONS

As you consider your own (as an educational leader) or your organization's commitment to DEI, which guiding question captures your attention the most and why?

Which guiding question represents a growth area for you and/or your school, district, nonprofit, or company?

> **Which guiding question represents an area of strength for you and/or your school, district, nonprofit, or company?**
>
>
>
>
>
>

SAMPLE NEXT STEPS

Here are example next steps you can take in this overall area of organizational clarity and commitment to DEI:

- As a school, network, district, nonprofit, or company, adopt a DEI toolkit or analysis resource to review your current school, district, nonprofit, or company's policies, practices, and procedures on a regular basis (including, but not limited to, budgeting, programmatic efforts, communications, recruitment and hiring, human resources, development, etc.).
- As a school, network, district, nonprofit, or company, establish a DEI working group or committee within your school, district, nonprofit, or company that regularly convenes to identify areas for professional learning, discuss pressing challenges and concerns related to DEI within the organization, progress monitor your racial equity action plan to ensure consistency and fidelity (follow-up and follow-through).
- As a school, network, district, nonprofit, or company, internally and externally share your DEI stance and/or commitment within your workplace, on your website, within your core internal documents (e.g., your handbook), on your social media handles, and all other places that apply for maximal internal and external visibility so that there is no ambiguity as to what your beliefs are, what your philosophy is, or what your overall commitment to DEI is.

CHAPTER 4

School Board Governance

Board governance is critically important as an area to embed DEI. Boards hold power, exercise oversight, steer the directionality of a school/network/district/org, and manage the chief executive officer, executive director, or president. If you're seeking to examine racial and other forms of injustice, harm, or oppression and the way they exist within the education sector, please don't skip examination of board governance.

In the midst of the pandemic, I wrote an opinion editorial that was published nationally on August 4, 2020. As a Black woman with educational leadership experience, having been a Black child growing up in poverty who attended an under-resourced public school system, I felt compelled to do so based on a few different concerning patterns I had begun to notice as it relates to both traditional elected and charter school board governance of predominantly Black schools within some of our country's most major metropolitan cities. It's reprinted here.

So, You Want to Run for School Board. First Ask Yourself If You Believe in the Genius of Black Children and Are You Willing to Fight to See It Realized

Publication Source: The 74

Written by Krystal Hardy Allen

Stewardship of anything is not a right, but rather a privilege. For every individual considering running for a school board seat within a traditional public school system, every individual contemplating joining a charter school board, and every current sitting school board member within either setting: This message is for you. In the height of our chants and demands to create a world where Black lives truly matter, I challenge you to examine the beliefs and assumptions you may hold about Black children, in particular, as you consider accepting positions to exercise governance of their public education.

At a moment in time when posting a #BlackLivesMatter message onto school, district or network social media platforms; crafting public statements; and even quickly providing Juneteenth as a paid day off can unfortunately also be driven by a leader or organization's commitment to optically or politically

(continued)

appear aligned (though often not aligned in its internal policies and practices), I believe it is critical to dig deep and recognize that far too many board members view Black children from a deficit-based lens.

To begin with, board members must believe that Black children—regardless of their economic status—are absolutely brilliant. In fact, Black children arrive to us in this state because they descend from a multitude of generations that have consistently modeled innovation in the worst of circumstances, beauty in the midst of deep generational pain, and problem-solving in the midst of hopelessness. Our children's minds are intricate, their thoughts are vast, and their audacious visions for the future have often paved the way to some of the most catalytic social change our country has ever seen.

As a board member, believe in their power. Ensure that educators within your district or network make it their mission to discover the brilliance they already possess, move mountains to provide them the resources they need to actualize their gifts, and make it a point to consistently enforce intentional language of their strengths and assets as opposed to consistent framing of the disparities they face.

Our children don't need saviors. Our children need leaders who will stand up for them and not be swayed by personal or political gain and interests. The question is: Do you really believe in the genius of Black children, or deep down, do you believe Black children—particularly those in poverty—are inferior and undeserving of the best? To the extent that you believe the latter, you will always allow and make excuses for the operation of schools that are unfit and the mismanagement of funds, and unequivocally provide an inferior education that reinforces the aspirations of white supremacy.

As a board member, you must also believe that Black children are undeniably multifaceted, multitalented, and far from being a monolith. When you believe this, you will fight for a plethora of rich learning opportunities, not subpar resources; access to a variety of content offerings, not just the bare minimum of what is required by your state; and you will do absolutely everything in your power to position and showcase the gifts, talents, creativity, and powerful individuality they bring, not only within your local landscape, but to a national and global stage.

Black children are incredibly resilient, inquisitive, and fascinating. They need not be told what a character trait of grit looks like because in far too many settings, many of our Black youth embody this character trait in more ways than the educators who stand in front of them. However, when you only see our children in stereotypes and do not believe or see the wealth of knowledge and assets within our community, you will never position yourself as a board member to center their voices nor the voices of our community in your decision-making.

Find any and every chance you can get to spend time with students and families within your district or network. Use your personal and professional resources to position our children for success versus only doing so for your own children. Understand that our children are your children. They're not "those children" or "these kids." Their mental, emotional, and physical well-being is your literal responsibility.

The question is: Do you believe that the Black children deserve absolutely everything you want for your own kids? Even for Black school board members, if your class, social status, affiliation with a sorority or fraternity, etc. compel you to believe that you and your children or family are better than the Black children and families you serve as a board member, you are also deeply a part of the problem. For any and all board members, whatever you do and want for your children should be no different than what you do for the children of the district and network you serve.

Penning this piece was a deeply meaningful, emotional, and internal process of birthing what I felt needed to be said in the midst of my observation of nepotism, classism, colorism, elitism, a lack of internal reflection and collective accountability, and other trends among school board members. It disgusted me. No one is perfect, but what I felt it spoke to and still speaks to is the following:

- The rarity of boards engaging in individual reflection and evaluation as a governing member
- How often or to what extent all boards conduct collective evaluation of their performance in the same way that they evaluate their superintendents or charter school CEOs and executive directors
- How many board members lack truly substantive DEI training
- The way that DEI is placed onto school-based leadership roles and positions as well as teaching and school-based staff positions as their responsibility, but is often not seen as work that boards are responsible for taking on and deeply engaging in themselves within their governance responsibilities, such as policy making

This entire chapter is devoted, therefore, to the very necessary work that school board members—whether they are traditional public school board members or charter school board members, whether they are elected or appointed—can engage in in order to center and advance DEI.

TWO DIRECTIONS OF THOUGHT

Let's first break down the fact that school board members should think of DEI within two different buckets. One bucket is devoted to deepening their understanding of what a diverse, inclusive, and equitable school or school system is, what it looks like, what it entails, and how to achieve it. Deepening their understanding in this area affects their ability to use a DEI lens work supporting and holding their school and/or system accountable to inclusive and equitable outcomes. One effect of a board member's ability to deepen their understanding of what DEI within a school or system entails is the shift in questions that are asked within board meetings to the superintendent, CEO, executive director, or school-based administrative representative present. Whereas a superintendent or comparable leader might provide, for instance, a report of the state of retention of staff members, particularly within what we know is a rapid increase in teacher turnover, and board members may hear a general number of the school or system's retention health, board members who have a developed a rich DEI lens may begin to do the following:

- Ask follow-up questions about whether there are major gender differences within the turnover of teachers within their school, system, or network.
- Ask follow-up questions about whether there are noticeable racial differences in the turnover of teachers within their school, system, or network.
- Inquire about whether the school, system, or network is collecting qualitative or quantitative data on the sense of belonging and other measures of inclusion and how that data is being used.
- Inquire about whether interventions or methods used to address teacher turnover are differentiated or whether they're enacting the same method across the board.

Overall, you cannot govern and lead a school, system, or network to achieve its mission and vision if you or we are not equipped with the knowledge of what a quality education encompasses. Creating a school environment for students and adults that is diverse, inclusive, and equitable *is* a key ingredient.

The second bucket that matters for school board members is their understanding of what DEI within each of their core board responsibilities looks like. This—for instance—includes how board members should approach board recruitment (for appointed roles), board culture, succession planning (for charter boards), policy making, committees, and more through a DEI lens or with DEI in mind. One effect of doing so would be the creation of a matrix for board-appointed members that encompasses more than professional backgrounds (e.g., accounting, law, medicine, fundraising, etc.) but also a DEI lens, so the board may also become more mindful of these issues:

- Socioeconomic diversity (in order to not fall into the trap of believing that to be a thriving appointed board, everyone must be wealthy, affluent, a high middle class earner, and so on—but instead recognizing and not discounting the social capital that board members

who may not have financial wealth themselves bring to the table as well as the connections and proximity people have to financial capital especially for fundraising purposes)
- Diversity in age (having different generations present on the board)
- Diversity in geographic origin (being mindful of who may be native to the city the school or organization operates within, being mindful of the different geographic neighborhoods or areas of a city board members may represent, reside in, or come from)

Similar to the section on Organizational Clarity and Commitment in Chapter 3, I provide a few examples of resources, tools, or frameworks that serve as sample levers for establishing your vision, goals, and strategies as it pertains to school board governance.

SAMPLE FRAMEWORK: NSBA

One tool I'd like to highlight is the National School Board Association's amazing 2021 "Reimagining School Board Leadership: Actions for Equity" toolkit. Here, you'll find an excerpt that's incredibly helpful for school board members:

> *NSBA recognizes that based on factors including but not limited to disability, race, ethnicity, and socioeconomic status, students are deprived of equitable educational opportunities. Fortunately for our students, demographics are not destiny. Operating with an equity lens empowers school board members to intentionally allocate resources, instruction, and opportunities according to need, requiring that discriminatory practices, prejudices, and beliefs be identified and eradicated.*

> ***Policies, programs, and curriculum must be audited for equity.***
> *School boards must understand that with equity, there is no such thing as neutral policies. They are either exacerbating, perpetuating, mitigating, or eliminating inequities.*

> ***School boards set visions and policy.***
> *Under today's rules of governance and best practices, the school board must take seriously its role to create a district culture that strives for excellence, acknowledges and addresses inequities, views mistakes as learning opportunities, and sees its work as one of constant improvement—looking ahead rather than behind. This is the time to partner with the professional educators to do everything we can to safeguard student learning. Every question should be asked in the tone and spirit of fiduciaries who are deeply committed to the mission, with a fail-forward mentality where information is data from which to learn, and questions are asked with a growth mindset.*

> ***School boards are empowered to be the guiding force for a district.***
> *They are uniquely positioned to drive change, and the need for that change has never been more apparent than now. Not just based on the obvious things that will change*

in terms of how they govern themselves but in a push for change found in the opportunity presented to do better. To meet the needs of every student, create safer learning environments, and act against institutional racism and inequities plaguing our country, boards must ask the right questions and then listen to what their stakeholders have to say. Boards must not wait to be told what their communities need but instead strive to find those answers and drive action themselves.

School board members have the positioning and power to employ the key levers to create more equitable outcomes.
We must ensure equity in school funding, ensure access to high-quality and high-level curriculum, ensure access to effective teachers, ensure safe and supportive school climates, and foster meaningful community engagement.

School board members have clear spheres of influence by which to effect necessary change.
Leadership—School boards set the tone for how the business of teaching and learning is carried out in their district. School boards lead by defining the mission, vision, and core values for the school district. Do the mission, vision, and core values of your district communicate a commitment to educational equity? School boards also lead by setting policy that clearly defines what they see as the priorities for daily management and implementation by the superintendent and staff. When policies are grounded in the needs of students and responsive to the local context of the district, equitable outcomes for students are more likely. Perhaps most importantly, school boards ensure that the values and priorities they have defined are reflected in the annual budget before approval.

Accountability—The board is responsible for ensuring that the superintendent and leadership team can execute on the vision and priorities that the board has established. Strong governance processes that facilitate healthy collaboration between the board and superintendent are vital. Transparent mechanisms for oversight are essential. As COVID-19 has undeniably demonstrated, delivering a world-class education to children in challenging circumstances requires flexibility and accountability. For school boards committed to equity, adaptive governance will continue to be the norm.

Community engagement and advocacy—School board members are a community's steward of its most precious resource—the future. Leading with an equity lens will create substantial change for the entire community, so boards should create avenues for listening and responding to community input. School districts can benefit when boards engage local entities, including service providers and industry as partners to help meet students' needs. As board members engage the community, it is important to reflect on your board's current makeup. Be aware of the ways your board does and does not reflect your community.

As you can tell from this snippet of content found within the toolkit, it is truly an incredible guide that school board members—regardless of type or school or geography context—can truly benefit from in helping them imagine and determine their own vision for DEI within their own governance responsibilities in addition to what they want to see within their schools as a whole.

SAMPLE FRAMEWORK: TEXAS ASSOCIATION OF SCHOOL BOARDS

Another tool I'd like to highlight is the work of The Texas Association of School Boards. They've published a beautiful article entitled "How to Start Addressing Equity, Diversity, and Inclusion in Our Schools." Check out the following excerpt.

Assess your situation

The promise of Texas public education should be that ZIP code, skin color, family background, and economic status are not a predictor of a student's success. While each of our students comes from different circumstances, this shouldn't limit our systems or our expectations for ensuring that every student is fully equipped for their life after high school.

As a locally elected school board member, you're key to making this a reality. Equity begins in the board room, and equity in learning and educational attainment is necessary for every student's lifelong success.

It's essential to understand the demographics of your district—both students and staff. Looking at the data can help your board identify trends in your district and community. It can help you ask informed questions about achievement patterns:

- *Where do different racial and ethnic students live in our community?*
- *What are the housing patterns and the history of these housing patterns?*
- *Which schools do these students attend?*
- *Which students participate in which programs?*
- *What is the racial makeup of various classes?*
- *Who is being identified for special education?*
- *Who participates in extracurricular activities and clubs?*
- *What are the attendance patterns and graduation rates for different groups?*
- *Which students are being disciplined most, in what ways, and why?*

The Intercultural Development Association recommends that school boards answer the following questions to begin assessing equity in serving all students:

- *How does this practice impact all learners?*
- *What policies, resources, and other support are needed to create equitability across different populations?*

- *What might create a negative or adverse impact on any identifiable population?*
- *How might that adverse impact be avoided?*
- *What precautions should we take as we move forward?*
- *How do we monitor our work to ensure comparable high outcomes for all students?*

Develop a plan with a clear vision

You have the tools to achieve more equitable outcomes. It begins with a clear vision for success that includes the success of each child. It causes us to develop—with input from the superintendent—clear, specific, and disaggregated goals for student performance.

In fact, the law now requires that we do this. While the governor provided a waiver of a few months for adopting HB 3 goals and plans, disaggregating data as a board and adopting specific goals for each of our student groups is still an essential governance practice and opportunity.

Monitor your progress

Having a compelling vision for each student's success and creating clear, specific goals for attaining that vision is a beginning. If we're going to be successful, we must monitor our progress along the way. Every single trustee in Texas needs to be able to answer three specific questions about equity in their district:

1. *How are the various diverse student groups doing in our district?*
2. *What are we doing to improve the learning of these different groups?*
3. *How will we know we are making progress and reaching our goals?*

Answering those questions accurately and with conviction requires us to use one of the most powerful tools in our toolkit: the power of the question. These are not close-ended gotcha questions, but rather open-ended curious questions.

Ask the superintendent how diverse student populations are doing in the district. The answer should inspire additional curious questions about specific groups:

- *How are the boys doing?*
- *How are the girls doing?*
- *How are the third graders at Eastside Elementary doing this year?*
- *What percentage of our ESL students were kindergarten ready this year?*
- *How are our eighth-grade algebra students doing this year?*
- *What percentage of African American and Hispanic students are taking AP classes this year?*
- *How does this compare to other students and what were our numbers last year?*

These questions are not intended to all be asked in one setting, but they are examples of the types of questions that have power—the power to shine light, the power to aid understanding, the power to guide action, the power to hold systems accountable.

Continuously refine your plans

Continue to ask good questions. They help us understand where we are and what we need to do to get where we want to go. For the governance team, the discussion that comes from good, informed questions can help us thoughtfully adjust our governance practices.

How diverse student populations are doing and what we are doing to support their improved learning should inform every decision your board makes and touch every aspect of governing:

- *Board agendas*
- *Monitoring plans*
- *Policy making*
- *Community engagement*
- *Budgeting priorities*
- *School boundaries*
- *Superintendent evaluation*
- *Transportation*

This should be an important part of every governance discussion, deliberation, and decision-making. To do anything else would be irresponsible. And this must be an ongoing part of the process.

Question the status quo to move forward

Question the status quo and work together with administrators to improve student success for every child. This starts with including a strong commitment to equity reflected in your district vision statement and goals. It could include a local equity policy that codifies values and commitment to equitable outcomes. It might involve self-reflection or assessment of programs, practices, and outcomes.

TASB is here to serve you and help you meet the needs of your students. We are actively working on new resources and services to assist districts that want to focus more attention on equity in student outcomes. This includes a collaborative approach from Legal Services, Policy Service, HR Services, Board Development Services, and other areas of TASB.

ADDITIONAL TOOLS

Here are additional frameworks, resources, and tools I recommend for your consideration · in the process of thinking through ways to build your awareness:

- The National School Board Association's "Reimagining School Board Leadership: Actions for Equity Supplemental Guide (Starting the Conversation)" (https://eric .ed.gov/?id=ED626159)
- Board Source's "The Handbook of Nonprofit Governance" (https://boardsource.org/ product/handbook-nonprofit-governance/)
- The Center for Nonprofit Resources' "Board Governance and Best Practice Checklist" (https://docplayer.net/18226605-Board-governance-and-best-practice-checklist.html)
- The National Charter School Resource Center's "Toolkit for Board Members" (https:// charterschoolcenter.ed.gov/resource/charter-school-governing-board-composition-toolkit-board-members)
- Education Board Partners' "Governance Best Practices for Highly Effective Charter School Boards" (https://edboards.org/resources)
- Michigan Association of School Boards' "Board of Education Governance Standards" (https://www.michigan.gov/-/media/Project/Websites/mde/2017/08/31/Item_B_R _Michigan_Board_of_Education_Governance_Standards_RD2.pdf?rev=c7f13d592d11 4b3cac20dbb9ff804d07)

GUIDING QUESTIONS

Though not exhaustive, here are some essential questions school board members and those who want to support and also hold school board members accountable to advancing DEI should ask themselves and their boards:

- How well are we cultivating a deeper understanding of the community or communities that we serve and bringing their perspectives, needs, feedback, and priorities into our strategic boardroom discussions?
- If we currently have an appointed board, what is the racial composition of our board?
- If we currently have an appointed board, what is the socioeconomic background of our appointed board?
- If we currently have an appointed board, what is the gender composition of our appointed board?
- If we currently have an appointed board, do any of our board members represent the backgrounds of the students and families we serve?

For instance, a school may be designated only for students with autism, and this might look like being intentional in having parents or families of students with autism on the board or board members who themselves have autism and are comfortable being advocates for and bringing the lens of experiences of students with autism.

- Is our school or organization's reputation being negatively (or positively) affected by our board's current composition?
- If we do not plan to have a board, will we operate an advisory board, hire an executive coach, or pursue a different means of ensuring sound, ongoing counsel in the areas of our blind spots?
- If someone were to make assumptions about our organizational values based on your current board composition, what would they be likely to think?
- How will you ensure that your founding board members are set up for success, particularly those from marginalized backgrounds?
- How will we or do we orient and onboard your new founding board members?
- How do we define highly effective board onboarding?
- Do you have detailed board role descriptions, bylaws, and other essential documents needed to provide maximum clarity to your founding board members?
- Do you have a board matrix that outlines the varying aspects of diversity (e.g., race, gender, geographic origin, industry, etc.) on your board?
- How will you orient and onboard your new founding board members?
- How will we or do we ensure that we are creating a welcoming and inclusive board culture?
- Are we ever at risk of making decisions without fully understanding how these decisions may affect those we serve?
- If we were to make a deeper commitment to DEI, what would that mean for our mission, our work, and the people we serve?
- How often do we engage in DEI training as a collective board?

Given these questions, let's think about how this applies to you. Next, I'd love you to reflect on a few questions about where your board is within their work and commitment to center DEI.

REFLECTION QUESTIONS

As you consider your own (as an educational leader) or your organization's board governance, which guiding question captures your attention the most and why?

Which guiding question represents a growth area for you and/or your school, district, nonprofit, or company's board?

Which guiding question represents an area of strength for you and/or your school, district, nonprofit, or company's board?

CASE STUDY: UPPER ARLINGTON SCHOOLS

Real-life case studies of the work are always incredibly helpful in painting a portrait of what is possible. In this section, I spotlight a Virginia school system's elected school board members engaged in the work and how their leadership in action helped to set the tone of all of the subsequent DEI work their district is currently engaged in doing. Let's first take note of their overall stance and reporting of work to date within the past few school years:

> *Upper Arlington Schools is committed to ensuring that our school district is a place where every member of our school community feels welcomed, valued, supported, and embraced.*
>
> *We believe it is our responsibility to teach and lead with diversity, inclusiveness, empathy, compassion, and civility, and provide our students, staff, and families with the tools to bring us together as one.*
>
> *Our vision is to challenge and support every student, every step of the way. As we move forward, we are committed to proactively responding to diversity, equity, and inclusion (DEI) needs in a manner that supports all students and creates a culture of safety and connectedness. We are committed to doing the work, as a community, in order to ensure that every student has a safe space to learn, grow and thrive without*

fear of prejudice or bias. We will examine our policies and practices to ensure that all facets of our school culture truly reflect our mission, vision, and values. We will seek to continuously raise awareness, develop understanding, and build skill through DEI programming and training opportunities.

The Upper Arlington Board of Education acknowledges that acts of racism, prejudice, bias, and bigotry occur within our schools and is committed to eliminating these experiences for students, families, and staff. We are committed to continue listening, learning, growing, and improving educational practices so that every child has a safe space to learn, grow, and thrive without fear of prejudice or bias. We are also committed to ensuring that diversity, equity, and inclusion and the related issues of student achievement and safety are top of mind at all times.

Under the leadership of the Board of Education, the district has taken the following steps:

Created an Equity Advisory Board to bring together the voices of students, staff, parents/guardians and community experts for guidance.

Created a new district-level leadership position for diversity, equity, and inclusion. Staff, student, and community feedback informed the selection process.

Created this section of our district website to share our commitment to our diversity, equity, and inclusion work and offer additional resources as they become available.

Ensured diversity, equity, and inclusion remain at the forefront by including an update in every Board of Education meeting and committee meeting.

Upper Arlington Schools is continuing to build on the diversity, equity, and inclusion work that we began in 2016 and the commitments we made in our strategic plan. Our focus on diversity, equity, and inclusion began in 2016 when the district partnered with the Upper Arlington Education Association and the Ohio Education Association to provide an unprecedented three-day training for more than 100 staff members from all areas of the district. These staff members now serve as leaders in diversity, equity, and inclusion work in their buildings and departments.

Our strategic plan builds on this foundation. Our strategic priority of student and staff well-being is rooted in our focus on diversity, equity, and inclusion. We believe it is essential for our students and staff to feel a sense of belonging and balance in order to have safe learning environments in which everyone can thrive. As we continue to focus on diversity, equity, and inclusion throughout the district, this page [district website] will contain links and information regarding our programming and other DEI resources to support students, staff, and our community.

Next, let's explore a sample resolution that this particular school board made in the name of moving the district forward in centering and advancing DEI:

Upper Arlington Schools Board of Education Resolution
June 16, 2020

Whereas, racism permeates every area of society in our country, including our schools; and

Whereas, it is incumbent upon all of us to fight to end racism and expose and address bias in our society; and

Whereas, Upper Arlington Schools adds its voice and resources to stand with those who have expressed the need for change; and

Whereas, we are committed to helping to find solutions that eliminate racism, social injustice, bias, and bigotry; and

Whereas, we further commit to continue listening, learning, growing, and improving educational practices so that every child has a safe space to learn, grow, and thrive without fear of prejudice or bias based upon race, color, ethnicity, or national origin; and

Whereas, we further commit to ensuring that diversity, equity, and inclusion and the related issues of student achievement and safety are top of mind at all times; and

Whereas, we further commit to diversifying our teaching and administrative staff, adding an executive director of diversity, equity, and inclusion, and creating an equity advisory board;

Whereas, it is our responsibility to teach and lead with diversity, inclusiveness, empathy, compassion, and civility; and

Whereas, we are committed to providing our students with the tools to leave behind what divides us, and bring us together as one; and

Therefore, the Upper Arlington Board of Education resolves to eliminate racism, social injustice, bias, and bigotry in our school community.

Last but not least, let's examine a bit of the origins of their work via their development of an Equity advisory board. Following, you can see the actual proposal they crafted that guided their work:

UPPER ARLINGTON SCHOOLS EQUITY ADVISORY BOARD PROPOSAL
JUNE 24, 2020
EQUITY ADVISORY BOARD PROPOSAL

INTRODUCTION

The Upper Arlington Board of Education acknowledges that acts of racism, prejudice, bias, and bigotry occur within our schools and is committed to eliminating these experiences for students, families, and staff. The 2019–2024 Strategic Plan recognizes the district's commitment to diversity, equity, and inclusion as an essential element of student and staff well-being. The Board of Education is committed to ensuring our schools are places where every student is welcomed, respected, celebrated, and supported while receiving the highest quality education.

To help further the district's work toward this goal, the Board of Education directed Superintendent Paul Imhoff, Ed.D., to create the Equity Advisory Board. The purpose of this Advisory Board is to utilize expert guidance and experience to create solutions in the areas of diversity, equity, and inclusion and to ensure the district continues to move forward in its commitment to all diversity, equity, and inclusion work.

STRUCTURE

The Advisory Board will play a supportive role in driving the diversity, equity, and inclusion priorities for the district. The Advisory Board will provide a level of expertise to the superintendent and the future executive director of diversity, equity, and inclusion, and will also work in conjunction with the building and district DEI teams. The Advisory Board will inform recommendations made by the superintendent to the Board of Education, which ultimately makes decisions regarding district policy and future direction.

The Advisory Board will also provide annual formal updates to the Board of Education and collaborate with the district on accountability data to be published in the Quality Profile and on the forthcoming Diversity, Equity, and Inclusion section of the district website, www.uaschools.org.

This volunteer group will be formed by the superintendent. It will be composed of committed individuals with a deep understanding of the importance and role equity plays in building a strong community. The Advisory Board will include 12 to 15 members, with representation from students, staff members, parents, and professionals in the field of diversity, equity, and inclusion. We anticipate the membership including:

- Three members of the teaching staff (elementary, middle, and high);
- One member of the classified staff;
- Two students;
- Six parents/guardians; and
- Three professionals in the field of diversity, equity, and inclusion.

In addition, the Board of Education president will annually appoint two members of the Board of Education to serve as liaisons to the Advisory Board. This group will meet monthly, with meetings facilitated by the executive director of diversity, equity, and inclusion. Terms and governance structures will be developed and set for the members of the advisory board.

TIMELINE

The superintendent will appoint a chairperson and co-chairperson for the Equity Advisory Board and work with them to recruit and review applicants against parameters designed to drive the overall goals and outcomes of the district's DEI strategy.

Interested individuals may submit a letter of interest and a resume detailing experience in the areas of diversity, equity and inclusion to Superintendent Paul Imhoff, Ed.D., by emailing superintendent@uaschools.org or by mail to 1950 North Mallway Drive, Upper Arlington, OH 43221. Applications will be due July 31, 2020.

Full Advisory Board membership will be established by the end of August 2020 with a first meeting in September 2020.

GOALS

Initially, the Equity Advisory Board will be charged with the goals listed below:

- *Identifying, gathering, and reviewing data to gain an understanding of the true student, staff, and family experience in the Upper Arlington community;*
- *Defining equity as it relates to the overall mission and strategic plan of the district;*
- *Supporting relationships with the City of Upper Arlington and other local public entities engaging in diversity, equity, and inclusion efforts;*
- *Building a sense of openness and safety in navigating uncomfortable conversations with and amongst the Upper Arlington community; and*
- *Providing insight and feedback on recruiting and retaining a diverse staff when job openings are available.*

We believe this initial work will provide an important foundation to guide the future work of the Equity Advisory Board as well as the district and building DEI teams.

CONCLUSION

The Equity Advisory Board will support the Board of Education's commitment to diversity, equity, and inclusion by sharing experience and providing expert guidance to the district's existing DEI teams and district leadership. This work will support the district's strategic plan and help us live up to our mission of challenging and supporting every student every step of the way.

Each of this school board's artifacts show examples of its work:

Establishing clarity of its why

Developing shared language

Developing their DEI vision

Determining what their DEI commitment would be

Communicating their DEI commitment

Its work investing their stakeholders in their DEI commitment

Developing a DEI plan (strategy)

Again, this case study or real-life example is not intended to be a perfect example of a DEI plan, but rather a clear example of how a group of educational leaders clearly define what is important to them, as well as how they will go about operationalizing their commitment to diversity, equity, and inclusion as a school community.

5

Organizational Leadership and Management

Effective school leadership is a vital component of the quality and overall success of any school or district. Organizational leadership within education influences the overarching vision for student outcomes that is established or the lack thereof. This includes leaders' ability to set the overall tone for a school or district's culture and climate—not just student culture and climate but adult culture and climate as well, and its interactions with families and communities. Muhammad Khalifa et al. (2016) indicate that culturally responsive leadership in schools requires that principals in particular lead in ways that promote practices that ask educators to engage in critical self-reflection and craft schools that engage and include all students.

As educational leaders increasingly express a desire to build an inclusive and equitable culture within their schools and districts, they also often face challenges in getting started or sustaining their work. Those challenges sometimes look like the following:

- **Uncertainty on where and how to start.** For instance, some predominantly white school or districts leaders may fear saying or doing the wrong thing so then take no action at all, which is perceived as being colorblind toward the experiences of people of color. Conversely, some leaders of color who have otherwise succeeded within white dominant cultures may fear being dismissed as too "passionate" if they raise concerns about DEI.
- **Lack of awareness of personal biases that inadvertently perpetuate harm within schools.** Often, educators—especially those who may consider themselves socially conscious, woke, anti-racist, or liberal in their views—may naturally view themselves completely prepared to engage in the work of DEI within schools though may not approach the work with a lens of self-examination, ownership, and accountability as opposed to a heavy hand on highlighting what the school or district is not doing to authentically operationalize DEI within schools. Nonetheless, even committed leaders—including people of color—can be unaware of the ways they themselves still contribute to harmful practices with children and peer adults.
- **Impatience with the depth and nonlinearity of the work required to build an inclusive and equitable school or district.** DEI work needs to go beyond the transactional—for instance, a focus on increasing "diverse" hires—to drive inclusion and equity. It requires embracing the challenges and tension that often accompany this work.

SAMPLE FRAMEWORK

One of my favorite frameworks for helping organizational leaders consider what the application of a DEI lens entails is the New York State Education Department (NYSED)'s "Culturally Responsive-Sustaining Education Framework." Check out the competencies it highlights for consideration for organizational leaders no matter your setting (i.e., schools, school districts, education nonprofits, and education companies). I want to highlight snippets from three different segments of this tool, which are its insights for school leaders, district leaders, and education department policy makers:

DEI Recommendations for School Leaders

Competency: Creating a Welcoming and Affirming Environment
Conduct periodic review of school policies (i.e. dress code, discipline code, conduct code), by collaborating with parents, teachers, community members, and incorporating research-based best practices such as restorative justice, positive behavior interventions, and supports.

Assess school climate using a variety of measures (i.e. surveys, interviews, focus groups, informal gatherings) to collect diverse stakeholder impressions and experiences, using questions that consider issues of diversity, equity, and inclusion.

Disaggregate data (i.e. discipline, attendance, enrollment in advanced coursework, special education, and gifted and talented programs) by sub-group, evaluate trends, and create a strategic plan to address disproportionality.

Provide space for teachers and staff to process and determine how to engage with students and families after social and political events that impact the wider community.

Support formal and informal structures for families to receive information about grade-level standards and expectations, developmentally appropriate social emotional tools, and strategies to support academic and social growth at home.

Provide interpretation services at family meetings (i.e., parent organization meetings, community events, during the enrollment process, during the provision of special education services, etc.) to ensure family engagement includes meaningful two-way communication and offers families the opportunity to share (not just receive) in their home language.

Develop multiple means of ongoing family engagement (i.e., apps and online systems of communication, parent leadership opportunities, parent family liaison positions, opportunities for families to serve as active co-creators of policies and programs, parent organizing bodies, and holding meetings at varied hours, possibly providing transportation and childcare, outreach at community meetings).

Create advisory groups consisting of various education stakeholders (families, teachers, students, community members) to work collaboratively to set school norms, establish school goals, and build alignment between the families' expectations and values, and the school's expectations and values.

Work with cultural and community centers to identify needs and provide services to families by offering classes such as parenting, financial literacy, computer literacy, or English language at the school.

Highlight works of art designed by students and members of the broader community that incorporate relevant cultural and historical context.

Create a visibly multilingual and multicultural environment by posting signs, banners, and other materials throughout the school that acknowledge and celebrate the identities of students.

Post high-quality work in the physical environment that is not limited to the display of correct answers, but also demonstrates students' critical thinking, conceptual understanding, reasoning, and application of content to meaningful real-world situations. Work to ensure high-quality work is equitably represented from students across sub-groups.

Create "listening conferences" or "peacemaking circles" led by a trained facilitator through which all stakeholders can discuss cultural and social values and resolve conflict.

Develop peer mediation programs where trained student mediators assist their peers in settling disputes.

Incorporate time in the school day when formal restorative practices can occur.

Provide the time and resources for students to create cultural clubs to learn more about their culture as well as other students' cultures.

Develop interview questions when hiring new staff that provide opportunities for candidates to identify ways they share (or don't share) experiences with the local student populations and to explain the implications of those experiences for their professional practices.

Incorporate parent and community voices into the hiring process.

Competency: Fostering High Expectations and Rigorous Instruction
Have high expectations and ensure rigorous instruction for all students regardless of identity markers, including race, gender, sexual orientation, language, ability, and economic background.

Reflect on your own implicit bias, how that bias might impact your expectations for student achievement or the decisions you make in the school, and the steps you can take to address your biases and their impact on students.

Develop in-school inquiry-based teams to address instructional rigor, cultural responsiveness, achievement disparities, and student engagement.

Embed cognitive and instructional strategies into teacher coaching that enables students to strengthen learning capacity.

Embed cognitive and instructional strategies into the teacher coaching model that pushes teachers to put the cognitive lift on students. Coach teachers to deliver high-quality instruction that enables students to grow as independent learners, think critically, make meaning of new concepts in multiple ways, and apply learning to meaningful, real-world situations.

Promote alternative achievement metrics that also support academics (e.g., demonstrating school values, strong attendance, leadership, growth).

I get so excited reviewing these insights of ways to center and advance DEI for school leaders (e.g., principals, assistant or vice principals, etc.) because of how practical, concrete, and necessary they are within K–12 settings! Now, let's take a look at a snippet of insights for district-level leaders with any type of school system be it public or private. Next, you'll find an excerpt from the New York State Education Department (NYSED)'s "Culturally Responsive-Sustaining Education Framework":

Recommendations for DISTRICT LEADERS

Competency: Fostering High Expectations and Rigorous Instruction
Strategize instructional methods to disrupt any disparities in student success outcomes that exist across lines of difference, highlighting and sharing best practices from the field.

Incorporate adaptive learning methods that encourage differentiation, exploration and curiosity as opposed to scripted, one-size-fits-all instructional programs.

Partner with experts in the field (i.e., professional learning organizations, higher education, consultants) to identify research-based, instructional strategies that are most effective in advancing student academic success.

Use tools to identify and recognize instructional methods that high-performing, culturally responsive-sustaining teachers are using across content areas.

Facilitate structures for teacher collaboration across school and district teams, i.e., peer observations, school visits, purposeful partnerships, mentor teachers.

Competency: Identifying Inclusive Curriculum and Assessment
Adopt curriculum that includes culturally authentic learning experiences that mirror students' ways of learning, understanding, communicating, and demonstrating curiosity and knowledge.

Adopt curriculum that highlights contributions and includes texts reflective of the diverse identities of students and reframes the monocultural framework that privileges the historically advantaged at the expense of other groups.

Invest in research to determine assessments geared toward academic achievement for underrepresented and underserved students of diverse identities.

Formally disseminate existing research on best practices from the field regarding culturally responsive-sustaining curriculum, instruction, and assessment to stakeholders in the district.

Partner with higher education institutions on curriculum development, coaching, and consultation around issues of diversity, equity, and inclusion (e.g., immigration, integration, diversification of curriculum).

Create courses district-wide about the diversity of cultures representative of the state of New York (e.g., Native Americans, African Americans, Latinx Studies, Asian

American Studies, Gender Studies) in a way that is comprehensive (e.g., across grade levels and not relegated to one specific month) and empowering (e.g., African American history does not begin with slavery, but with African history).

Last but not least, let's check out a snippet of The New York State Education Department (NYSED)'s Culturally Responsive-Sustaining Education Framework's insights for education department policy makers, which is really essential yet rare to find for policy makers. Similar to every other domain of DEI operationalization we explore in this text, this is simply one example of a framework you can use to imagine and drive your understanding of what centering DEI within organizational leadership and management includes. The following is an excerpt from the New York State Education Department (NYSED)'s "Culturally Responsive-Sustaining Education Framework":

Recommendations for EDUCATION DEPARTMENT POLICYMAKERS

Competency: Engaging in Ongoing Professional Learning and Support
Build internal staff capacity to engage in continuous professional learning and growth around culturally responsive sustaining practices that will be reflected in policies.

Provide supports, opportunities, and resources that build stakeholders' capacity to implement CR-S practices.

Continuously engage staff members in professional learning about implicit bias, with particular attention to allowing staff members to identify and challenge their own biases, and training them on identifying and addressing implicit bias in the workplace.

Provide educators with opportunities for professional learning in the areas of equity, anti-bias, multicultural, and culturally responsive-sustaining pedagogies.

Identify and share research practices proven effective and highlight examples of best practices from the field.

Competency: Creating a Welcoming and Affirming Environment
Strive to be sustaining by centering the identities of all students in our educational policies, encouraging cultural pluralism rather than creating policies that ask students to minimize their identities in order to be successful.

Strive to be responsive to the needs of students, teachers, school and district leaders, parents, and families.

Work to expand the recruitment and retention of a diverse staff with identities and experiences that reflect the varied experiences of the student population in New York State (i.e., staff who identify as people of color, LGBTQIA+, differently abled; staff with experience in both rural and urban populations).

Make accessible and readable information readily available, in multiple languages, to parents and families.

Develop guidance on ways schools can respond to local and global events, as well as prominent community concerns.

Provide resources families need to be engaged advocates for their children's sense of belonging in school, with particular regard to the opportunities and challenges associated with having marginalized identity markers (i.e., race, sexuality, gender identity, ability, language, etc.).

Recognize the effect of school environment on student achievement and continue to expand the development of tools that assess, address, and support the improvement of school climate.

Engage families and communities in a respectful way.

GUIDING QUESTIONS

Here are some essential questions I believe school and district leaders should ask in first examining where their school or district lies in relationship to leading for equity:

- Does the principal/executive director/CEO/president, departmental leaders, and/or each member of the leadership team demonstrate an understanding of the impact of systems of oppression (racism, sexism, etc.)? If so, how do we know?
- How is cultural competency defined and evaluated for leaders? What tools are used? How often and by whom?
- Does the school, district, nonprofit, or company leader or manager actively seek to develop cultural competency? If so, how? In what formal ways?
- What is the racial/ethnic composition of your school, district, nonprofit, or company's leadership team?
- What is the gender composition of your school, district, nonprofit, or company's leadership team?
- What are the various other forms of social identity that are or are not represented within your school, district, nonprofit, or company's leadership team?
- What is the racial/ethnic composition of middle leaders (that may or may not be formal members of your school, district, nonprofit, or company's leadership team)?
- What other forms of social identity are represented within your school, district, nonprofit, or company's middle leadership team?
- Are people of color (and other marginalized groups) in positions of power and key decision-making within your school, district, nonprofit, or company's leadership team?
- Do they have real, actual power or symbolic power?
- Who makes what decisions?
- Who is at the table, and who is not?
- To what extent is there a spoken or unspoken archetype of what a leader looks like, sounds like, and so on within your school, district, nonprofit, or company?
- To what degree is this type grounded in assimilation and other forms of the dominant culture?

- Who has access to what information within your school, district, nonprofit, or company?
- What determinants drive who has access to what information within your school, district, nonprofit, or company?
- What formal ways do you ensure that all voices, input, and perspectives are valued and appreciated within your school, district, nonprofit, or company?
- In your school, district, nonprofit, or company, is there a decision-making matrix in place?
- If so, who constructed it? Was it vetted by a diverse group of stakeholders within the organization?
- If so, does it include an explicit racial, gender, socioeconomic, or other lens of questioning who your school, district, nonprofit, or company's policies and practices intentionally or unintentionally advantage? Disadvantage?
- Within your school, district, nonprofit, or company, who is at an inherent advantage within a particular policy or practice?
- Who is at an inherent disadvantage within a particular policy or practice within your school, district, nonprofit, or company?
- To whose values does your school, district, nonprofit, or company subscribe?
- Is there an emphasis on a dominant group's values that by default is thus not inclusive to others within your school, district, nonprofit, or company?
- Is there a formal means of understanding and evaluating the experiences of Black and Brown (and other marginalized groups) organizational leadership team members in your school, district, nonprofit, or company? What about your middle leaders?
- How often is such information formally gathered and analyzed by your school, district, nonprofit, or company?
- What actions are and have been taken as a result of the experiences of Black and Brown (and other marginalized groups) leaders within your school, district, nonprofit, or company?
- Does the leadership team within your school, district, nonprofit, or company model comfort with leading conversations about race, gender, privilege, power, and so on ?
- Is undue burden placed on Black and Brown leaders (or members of other marginalized groups) of your school, district, nonprofit, or company to lead and guide conversations and initiatives regarding race for your school, district, nonprofit, or company?
- Does the leadership team of your school, district, nonprofit, or company create an environment that facilitates productive dialogue about race (and other forms of social identity) and lays a foundation for action?
- Does the leadership team of your school, district, nonprofit, or company welcome and accept feedback related to matters of DEI from a variety of perspectives?
- If so, how? How often?
- What action is taken with the collection of such information?

■ Within your school, district, nonprofit, or company, does the leadership team ensure that your school, district, nonprofit, or company establishes explicit, annual DEI goals across varying roles and domains of operation, as well as action plans that drive your school, district, nonprofit, or company's ability to reach its goals?

Given these questions, let's think about how this applies to you using the reflection questions.

REFLECTION QUESTIONS

Which guiding questions capture your attention the most and why?

Which guiding question represents a growth area for you and/or your school, district, nonprofit, or company?

Which guiding question represents an area of strength for you and/or your school, district, nonprofit, or company?

SAMPLE NEXT STEPS

Though not in any way exhaustive, here are sample next steps school, system, and organizational leaders can take in this area:

- As a school, network, district, nonprofit, or company, ensure that every leadership team member of your school, district, nonprofit, or company attends relevant DEI training on an ongoing basis and shares their learnings and/or next steps transparently with the rest of the organization for transparency and collective accountability.
- As a school, network, district, nonprofit, or company, build a formal racial equity or general DEI action plan that outlines your concrete priorities, goals, strategies, and who owns what (who is responsible for what).
- As a school, network, district, nonprofit, or company, conduct a DEI audit of particular domains of your school, district, nonprofit, or company as a whole to develop a deeper understanding of your strengths, weaknesses, opportunities, and threats.
- As a school, network, district, nonprofit, or company, adopt an equity toolkit or analysis tool to review policies, practices, and procedures on a regular basis (including, but not limited to budgeting, programmatic efforts, communications, recruitment and hiring, human resources, development, etc.) of your school, district, nonprofit, or company.
- As a school, network, district, nonprofit, or company, establish a DEI working group or committee within your school, district, nonprofit, or company that regularly convenes to identify areas for professional learning, discuss pressing challenges and concerns related to DEI within your school, district, nonprofit, or company, as well as progress monitor your equity action plan to ensure consistency and fidelity (follow-up and follow-through).

6

Human Resources (HR)

Human resources (HR) is a vital part of centering and advancing DEI. The following areas and ways are important to consider when centering DEI within HR:

- Compensation & benefits
- Talent recruitment
- Interviewing and hiring (selection)
- Onboarding
- HR information systems (including data and analytics)
- Professional development
- Performance management
- Staff culture and climate
- Succession planning
- Offboarding

Let me give you one example of an HR-related matter that reveals the need for using an intentional lens of DEI within HR. We often see school systems put forth a great deal of money to recruit teachers and administrators of color. However, unfortunately, the retention of that same demographic isn't good or strong because the focus is on creating the optics and perks of attracting people into the work, but not on creating and maintaining the right conditions that ensure those employees are fairly treated, properly supported, work in respectful and psychologically and emotionally safe work conditions, and more, that will *keep* them there. In other words:

- Hiring more Black and Brown staff members means nothing if you can't retain them.
- Hiring more women means nothing if you don't respect them.
- Members of marginalized communities are not props, toys, or tokens.
- When you learn to honor who people are and create the right conditions and spaces for them, you won't have to worry about finding them or keeping them.

There is a deep relationship between the conditions you create for staff members and your ability to attract as well as retain talent. If the environment isn't right, you can't possibly expect people to desire staying within a space that is harmful mentally, emotionally, physically, or spiritually for them. This also holds true for organizational spaces that are simply stagnant and/or resistant to change.

When I reflect on some of my own experiences as a Black teacher, middle leader (i.e., an assistant principal), and a principal who is also a woman, there are seven things I am hyper-aware staff members from marginalized communities are absolutely tired of:

- Not being listened to
- Not being paid for our intellectual labor
- Being overqualified and more knowledgeable than some leaders and managers within our districts, networks, nonprofits, and companies
- Performative statements and surface-level equity work
- Leaders who represent membership within marginalized communities themselves too but who are puppets of inequitable practices
- Being asked to engage in work with absolutely no acknowledgment of the social, emotional, and mental impacts of current-day traumas (e.g., racialized hate crimes like George Floyd's murder or the Asian American hate crimes that took place in Atlanta, Georgia, during the pandemic) we face

Even when we think about the culture and climate of the spaces we create for adults within the education field, we cannot prioritize the mental, social, and emotional well-being of children and ignore all those same needs for the educators who stand in front of them day after day. As educational leaders, we must stop thinking that the adults within our departments and building are perfectly fine because they look or appear to be fine, or because we simply carry the well-being of adults as an afterthought. We cannot think that adults within our educational systems, nonprofits, and companies will figure it out on their own.

The process of determining the needs of educators and educational leaders is not always, and won't ever always be, easy or smooth or quick, but it is the right thing to do. Perfection is not the point or goal, but if you're a board member, superintendent, executive director, chief executive officer, principal, head of school, or in any type of administrative position, the reality is that you and your school will hurt or feel the consequences in both the short and long term if you do not address and also prioritize the well-being (especially mental and emotional) of your employees in a meaningful—not cosmetic or superficial—way. This might mean fostering an intentional new partnership with a community organization to provide increased counseling and therapy offerings for staff members to address a heightened noticing of mental health challenges they may be facing.

This might mean or look like providing additional PTO time when possible. It may mean creating more planning and break times within the day for staff members as opposed to planning how you will use every single minute of their day's planning period for something else. All of these are meatier actions to take as opposed to providing a staff team pizza four times a year as a surprise. Although food is great and appreciated, fast food surprises are no substitute for addressing the daily, weekly, and monthly systemic matters—such as fatigue, burnout, turnover, helplessness, anxiety, frustration, and more—that teachers, noninstructional staff members, and leaders face every single day.

We have to consider adult psychology, human physiology, and other forms of medical science, but most important center the obvious signs and messages educators are sending leaders and decision-makers daily that are not paid attention to, listened to, or believed. Moral of the story: pay attention. Listen. Believe. Reflect. Discuss. Envision. Plan. Execute.

At a time when there is tremendous turnover or churn of teachers as well as leaders within the field of education, decision-makers have to adopt a lens of DEI in order to accurately diagnose the root causes of why staff members are leaving, as well as generate aligned solutions that ensure that working conditions within schools are equitable, inclusive, and set staff members up to thrive.

CASE STUDY: PRE- AND POST-KATRINA NEW ORLEANS

New Orleans's public education system is one of the most intriguing educational ecosystems in the United States, primarily due to its volume of drastic change, notably the ways in which urban education reform has served as the guiding post of the structures, systems, policies, and practices enacted within the modern-day New Orleans Public Schools system. Affectionately coined "The Big Easy," New Orleans, Louisiana, stands as our nation's first 100% charter school district. This phenomenon is the product of a series of events that transpired over time, including the catastrophic Hurricane Katrina that hit New Orleans on August 29, 2005. In the wake of Hurricane Katrina, thousands of employees—mostly Black teachers, principals, and other educational roles—were fired, the district's collective bargaining agreement expired, never to be renewed, and all New Orleans public school educators became at-will employees. This occurrence stands as one of the single most influential decisions that not only shifted an entire demographic's livelihood (i.e., that of the local Black middle class) but also fractured the fabric of racial representation in the education workforce in alignment to that of the students it served.

This occurrence was part of an effort led by varying leaders, such as elected officials, external education reform influencers, and local education reformers, to reinvent the city's school landscape. Prior to Hurricane Katrina, more than 80% of school administrators were Black, while the immediate years following the storm, demographics show what became a predominantly White-led educational system. Many educators were not rehired after the mass firing. Because of this sudden phenomenon of unemployment, varying forms of distress, and stigmatization through being labeled as "low-performing practitioners" by many local and national proponents of education reform at that time, an entire generation of Black educators and their families, as well as the entire middle class of Black New Orleans, suffered in ways that some have still been unable to recover from today. In "When Reforming Education Means Destroying Communities," Bruce Dixon (2010) states, "The current wave of what's called school reform replaced well-paid and experienced teachers, again overwhelmingly women and minorities, with a younger, Whiter, less well-paid workforce with few ties to the communities where schools are located."

In the aftermath of post-Katrina education reforms, far fewer teachers working in schools were born and raised in New Orleans, resulting in large cultural gaps (to say the least) between teachers and their majority Black, native New Orleanian students. Additionally, the level of experience of both teachers and administrators declined in the establishment of a new, radically different system of conversion to what would ultimately be an all-charter system, which prioritized teacher recruitment from alternative teaching programs, the disbanding of collective bargaining and protections, and more.

Why does this context matter? This all matters because it paints a portrait of the ways in which institutional and structural racism, lack of prioritizing family and community voice, and fundamental misalignment in having a shared vision for the purpose of education itself—particularly for Black children (as the majority of New Orleans students have been and still are)—have shaped the current public education landscape in New Orleans. Although there are certainly really great attributes to the current system, there are also major challenges within it. I share this case study because it depicts several different intersections of HR and how diversity and equity should be at the forefront of our HR decision-making.

SAMPLE FRAMEWORK: SUPPORTING TRANSGENDER EMPLOYEES

Let's check out the work of the Employers Council's 2021 "Employer Guide to Diversity, Equity, and Inclusion." Following, you'll find excerpts that HR leaders within our field of education should definitely consider.

Eliminating Barriers in the Workplace for Transgender Employees
WRITTEN BY LORRIE RAY, ESQ., SPHR, DIRECTOR OF MEMBERSHIP ENGAGEMENT

Documentation
In this context, the question frequently arises of what to do when an employee begins using a name that is different than their legal name, especially when the name is indicative of a different gender. To mitigate the risk of litigation in states where transgender status is protected by law, employers and coworkers should consider using the name and pronouns that the employee prefers. Employers may also want to consider updating business cards, nameplates, and email addresses to reflect the employee's chosen name. In states like Colorado and California, for example, the failure to use the pronouns associated with an employee's gender identity is considered unlawful discrimination.

Though employees may be entitled to the use of their chosen name in the workplace, the question still remains as to what name should appear on business documentation. Employers should generally use the employee's legal name for business documentation, such as personnel files, I-9 documentation, and payroll. This applies even when that name is inconsistent with the employees' preferred gender. If the employee chooses to change their name legally, employers should then update their documentation to reflect the employee's chosen name. In other words, employers should be mindful that federal agencies (like the Internal Revenue Service) have strict requirements when it comes to use of an employee's "legal name" that cannot be circumvented by the preferences of that employee. Failure to abide by these restrictions may even result in liability for the employer.

Bathrooms

Since workplaces commonly have separate bathrooms for men and women, employers may have questions about bathroom access for transgender employees. In many states with protections for transgender employees, these employees are required to have access to restrooms that correspond to their gender identity, even if it is different than their sex at birth. Indeed, these rules typically do not apply just to bathroom, but all gender-segregated facilities. It is important for employers to understand the regulations in the states in which they conduct business.

Employers may face a situation where one employee is uncomfortable sharing a restroom with a coworker who is transgender. Many states with protections for transgender workers hold that employers cannot question or ask an employee about their transgender status regarding bathroom choice. In these states, the discomfort of the coworker is usually outweighed by the legal or regulatory freedom of the transgender employee with respect to bathroom selection. One potential solution to this situation could be to allow the uncomfortable employee to use a restroom away from their typical work location. Some employers have implemented greater access to single user, unisex bathrooms, where possible, to avoid or resolve this issue.

Dress Code

Another question employers may face is how to enforce the dress code as it relates to a transgender employee. Typically, transgender employees will assume the appearance and dress of their preferred gender. Employers are generally allowed by the laws in states that prohibit discrimination based on transgender status to impose a dress code that is reasonable and serves a business purpose. Employers may face an issue if they have gender-specific dress codes. Generally, it is recommended, in accordance with those state laws, that employees apply dress codes consistently between the preferred gender of the transgender employee and other employees of that same gender. This means that employers should not, given state law, require a transgender employee to dress in a way that would be inconsistent with their gender identity.

REFLECTION QUESTION

> **What do you notice in this sample framework? What is most pronounced?**

SAMPLE FRAMEWORK: REDUCING INTERVIEW BIAS

Now, let's check out the work of the Employers Council's "2021 Employer Guide to Diversity, Equity, and Inclusion" regarding reducing. Following, you'll find excerpts that HR leaders within our field of education should definitely consider.

Beth Brown, SPHR, RPA, CEBS, Human Resources Consultant, Integrated Human Capital Services

Workplace diversity helps strengthen organizations and make them more successful. Reducing interview bias is an essential step in achieving a more diverse workforce. Many managers take an unstructured approach to interviewing, using conversation to allow information about the candidate's experience and expertise to come forward. While this tactic may feel comfortable, unstructured interviews are not a good indicator of a candidate's potential for success on the job. Instead, structured interviews, with each candidate being asked the same set of questions, help standardize the process, minimize bias, and ensure greater on-the-job success. In a structured process, employers can focus on the factors that directly impact successful performance.

Here are suggestions on creating and using a structured interview process:

First, understand the requirements of the job before the interview. Review the job description and position goals to clarify the skills and behaviors needed to be successful in the job.

Create a standard set of interview questions to ask all candidates. Concentrate on work history and job-related accomplishments and how they achieved them. Ask how the candidate would solve specific on-the-job problems, to learn their approach to work, understand their level of technical skill, and gain insight on their expectations for interacting with others to accomplish job goals. Using scripted questions allows for clearer comparisons between all candidates.

Consider a phone screen conversation before an in-person interview, using shortened questions from your interview script. This conversation can help reduce first impression bias.

Have interviewers note the candidate's answers immediately during the interview. This provides a more complete picture of the information provided by the candidate. Noting responses later, even immediately after the interview, can result in information gaps and recalling only dramatic examples. To make notetaking feel less awkward, explain to the candidate that the interviewers believe the interview is essential, and want to accurately remember what is said, so they will be taking notes during the interview.

Conduct a live debriefing session with all interviewers to share the information learned from the candidate. Comparing the candidates' responses "horizontally" across each question allows interviewers to see the strengths and weaknesses of the answers provided. For example, if you interview three candidates, compare all three candidates' answers to question one, then question two, and so on. This can make it easier to see the strongest candidate based on each question and is particularly helpful if the interview questions are weighted based on success in the job.

Iris Bohnet, Albert Pratt Professor of Business and Government, co-director of the Women and Public Policy Program and the academic dean at Harvard Kennedy School, in her April 18, 2016, article for *Harvard Business Review* entitled "How to Take the Bias Out of Interviews," explains that structured interviews can be taken even further:

Structured interviews are not just about discipline in asking questions—some companies, including Google, structure the content of their interviews using data. Their people-analytics departments crunch data to find out which interview questions are more highly correlated with on-the-job success. A candidate's superb answer on such questions can give the evaluator a clue about their future performance, so it makes sense that responses to those questions receive additional weight.

Using structured interviews, asking work situation questions, and doing comparative evaluations of candidate's answers all can help your organization choose a candidate with a good chance of success in the position while reducing bias in hiring.

REFLECTION QUESTION

What do you notice in the sample framework above? What is most pronounced?

CASE STUDY: MINNEAPOLIS PUBLIC SCHOOLS

Here is an excerpt that highlights work from Minneapolis Public Schools. This is an executive summary of their "Human Resources Equity and Diversity Impact Assessment" that was published in November 2018.

During the summer of 2017, the Board of Education directed the Accountability, Research, and Equity (ARE) Division to identify and examine inequities in Human Resources' (HR) policies, practices, and procedures through the Equity and Diversity Impact Assessment (EDIA). This EDIA examined the extent to which HR's policies, practices, and procedures influence the recruitment, hiring, and retention of effective teachers of color. ARE worked in partnership with the MPS HR Division and the EDIA Committee to complete the HR EDIA.

The HR Division is composed of four departments: Talent Acquisition, Talent Management, Employee Relations, and Human Resources Information Systems (HRIS). The Talent Acquisition team is responsible for identifying, attracting, and on-boarding top talent, and the Talent Management team oversees performance management and Quality Compensation (Q Comp). Employee Relations focuses on discipline, grievances, contract administration, and contract negotiations. Finally, the HRIS team is responsible for maintaining HR's personnel data and systems.

Preliminary findings were presented to the Board of Education on February 27, 2018, which were:

Finding 1—MPS has access to a limited pool of teacher candidates of color. Stakeholders identified two barriers contributing to MPS' limited pool of candidates of color: systemic barriers and passive recruitment strategies.

Passive Recruitment Strategies

- *Rather than actively seeking teacher candidates of color, Human Resources recruits more passively, relying on local career fairs, job search websites, university partnerships, and the "MPS community." Few school leaders recruit teacher candidates, for they feel recruitment is the responsibility of the Human Resources Department. Nevertheless, teachers of color are frustrated by MPS' passive approach, for they feel it conveys a lack of commitment to hiring racially and ethnically diverse candidates.*

Systemic Barriers

- *Both Human Resources and school leaders feel that largely white teacher preparation programs play a role in MPS' inability to recruit teacher candidates of color. Human Resources, school leaders, and teachers of color also acknowledge the impact of Minnesota's rigid licensure requirements, which may prevent people of color from securing teaching positions both in MPS and across the state.*

Finding 2—Teacher candidates of color face an uphill battle in hiring due to District and contractual policies and practices. The hiring process is challenging for Human Resources, school leaders, and teachers alike, largely due to certain contractual obligations and District hiring practices.

Contractual Obligations

■ *Certain contractual obligations, particularly those associated with the internal hiring process, unintentionally create obstacles for teachers of color; these obstacles are evident to both school leaders and Human Resources. The internal hiring process—including seniority, Interview and Select, and Matching—prevents Human Resources from posting most positions externally, leaving MPS' largely white workforce in place. The internal hiring process also poses challenges for school leaders, who feel unable to "shield" their less senior teachers of color during budget cuts, are frustrated by the ways in which Interview and Select delays Human Resources' hiring timeline, and feel that Matching prevents them from intentionally hiring staff to meet their buildings' needs.*

Hiring Practices

■ *Hiring is a decentralized process in MPS. Whereas Human Resources is responsible for managing vacancies, screening applicants, and submitting official offers, school leaders are responsible for conducting interviews and selecting acceptable candidates. School leaders found this process to be problematic, for they feel that Human Resources' hiring timeline is slow and their communication is lacking. Teachers of color were also challenged by Human Resources' lacking communication, and desired additional support navigating the system through the hiring process.*

Teacher Experience

■ *Once they are hired, teachers of color endure a challenging work environment. Teachers face persistent negative interactions, isolation, and bias—ranging from microaggressions to more serious behaviors—from colleagues, leaders, and the larger school community alike. Neither school leaders nor Human Resources are able to provide teachers with sufficient technical or adaptive supports, making them feel unsupported and unwelcomed. When teachers of color attempt to confront these inequities, they feel silenced and targeted, an experience that is only enhanced among non-tenured staff. Ultimately, these negative experiences and interactions have a compounding and detrimental effect on teachers' personal and professional well-being and success.*

Finding 3—MPS Teachers of color endure a challenging work environment. Teachers of color endure a challenging environment at MPS, characterized by persistent negative interactions, isolation, insufficient technical and adaptive supports, and job insecurity.

Job Insecurity

- *Teachers of color feel targeted by their colleagues—and, in some cases, school leaders—when they "speak their truth" to confront bias and inequity in their buildings. These feelings are enhanced among teachers who do not yet have tenure, as they are more likely to be exceeded during the budget tie-out process. Ultimately, teachers' lived experiences intersect with the weight of certain contractual obligations, and produce a sense of job insecurity among many teachers of color across MPS. School leaders know that teachers of color feel targeted by their colleagues. School leaders agree that certain contractual obligations create job insecurity among many teachers of color, and often struggle to "shield" these staff.*

Persistent Negative Interactions

- *Teachers of color feel they are assigned different, and sometimes additional, roles based on their race or ethnicity; this includes being directed to High Priority schools, being responsible for teaching "tough" students of color, and/or taking on the role of Behavior Dean. Teachers of color also feel as though they are held to a different standard than their white colleagues, while simultaneously receiving messages that they are not meeting these expectations. Finally, teachers experience consistent negative interactions with the school community; these interactions range from microaggressions to more serious forms of bias. Human Resources and school leaders are aware of these issues. Although some leaders are working to address this challenging climate, their efforts are not always well received by the school community.*

Isolation

- *Because they work in racially isolated spaces, teachers of color often feel excluded and unwelcome in their buildings. Given these persistent, negative, and exclusionary interactions, many teachers of color feel responsible for modeling respectful and inclusive interactions with their white colleagues. Ultimately, these experiences perpetuate teachers' feelings of isolation in the workplace. School leaders are aware that their teachers of color are isolated, and see connections between the building demographics and the intensity of teachers' feelings.*

Insufficient Technical Supports

- *Teachers of color, school leaders, and Human Resources are challenged by MPS' limited ability to offer technical supports. Human Resources provides basic, standardized information to new teachers, but leans on school leaders to provide more detailed, site-specific information. Both teachers of color and school leaders were dissatisfied with this onboarding process; teachers of color found the process to be limited in scope and poorly timed, and school leaders found the District's system to be insufficient in preparing new staff for their roles. Human Resources does not provide training or resources designed specifically for teachers of color. School leaders are challenged by these limited opportunities, as they feel teachers of color require additional training that they cannot provide.*

Insufficient Adaptive Supports

■ *Teachers of color feel unsupported by their leaders, though some teachers feel that the district, rather than their leader, is to blame. Neither HR nor school leaders feel that they are able to provide teachers of color with sufficient adaptive resources, or supports to navigate systems and structures. HR provides training and resources for school-based leadership teams (e.g., equity and engagement), expecting these teams to bring relevant information to their staff members.*

Retention and Exit

■ *The compounding effect of teachers' negative experiences makes them feel that MPS is an unwelcoming place to work. This leaves teachers at a professional crossroads: they can either (A) remain in their building in hopes it will improve, (B) remain in the District but take on a new role in a new building, or (C) exit the District entirely. Teachers who choose to remain in their building may face the same challenging environment they have in the past. Similarly, teachers who choose to stay with MPS but hope to transfer buildings must complete the hiring process again knowing that they may still face similar, negative experiences both during hiring and in their new site. Ultimately, this challenging cycle makes it more difficult for MPS to retain teachers of color.*

　　Finding 4—The compounding effect of these negative experiences makes MPS an unwelcoming place to work. Teachers' overwhelmingly negative experiences in the District make it challenging for MPS to retain teachers of color.

Teacher Retention

■ *Many teachers of color feel that MPS' white dominant culture discredits the ways they think and act. Teachers of color also question MPS' commitment to equity and diversity. These negative feelings and experiences have a compounding and detrimental effect on teachers' satisfaction and well-being, driving them to leave their site, and sometimes, the District. Regardless of their personal feelings, however, teachers are overwhelmingly concerned about how these dynamics harm the student experience. Though both District and site-based retention rates are high, retention rates are noticeably lower among teachers of color. Both school leaders and*

Human Resources are aware of these trends. School leaders feel that their teachers' inability to be their whole selves at work makes it challenging to retain them. Human Resources feels largely unable to support teacher retention because of the decentralized nature of their work. Instead, Human Resources believes staff retention is dependent on department and school leaders.

Although these findings describe the state of HR—including staff culture and climate— within Minneapolis Public Schools, these findings resound in being true and the reality for many other teachers of color across our country every single day.

As a Black school principal leading a campus of nearly 98% Black children during the time of the tragic murders of Alton Sterling in Baton Rouge, Louisiana, as well as Michael Brown in Ferguson, Missouri, I vividly remember feeling led to create authentic dialogue spaces for our upper elementary as well as our middle school students to process what was happening in the world around them. I remember being excited to open spaces in which we centered the question "What does it mean to be Black in America" to young people who truly had something to say. While my zeal as a native resident of historic Selma, Alabama, with its rich history of Black heritage, of pride, of social justice, and activism was no surprise to those who intimately knew me as Krystal the person, my work leading culturally responsive practices was not met with the warm embrace one would think particularly at that time. Instead, I experienced the following:

- The often private whispers of some white teachers and middle leaders who expressed discomfort with "the kinds of conversations she is bringing up with kids"
- Formal and informal complaints of those staff members to my superiors naming racial discourse opportunities with students to be things that made them feel uncomfortable and things they believed were not appropriate to discuss with young people in an elementary or middle school setting
- A supervisor (a charter management organization leader) sharing that the initiatives I planned and led "were simply best to stay away from doing," which at that time was a planned field trip to my hometown of Selma, Alabama, for its annual Bridge Crossing Jubilee that commemorates Bloody Sunday to meet icon Congressman John Lewis at the time and as well as a St. Louis trip to meet Michael Brown's father and learn from community leaders there about what bringing social change to their community means and what it looks like

As a Black woman principal, this meant that I didn't get the full support I needed for culturally responsive programming the way our campus needed. It means that I worked around my network or district at the time to find press opportunities for positive media coverage of the work we were doing in order to secure help—especially financial resources—for the social justice work we endeavored to provide students. Interestingly, but not surprisingly, positive media mentions would gladly be shared by our charter school network at the time, which is seemingly positive external support, yet I paid for it behind closed doors in not being consistently supported as I needed to be particularly when I spoke up about things I didn't believe in or felt were not right. My mind always goes back to those days and ultimately poor organizational leadership and management experiences I was on the receiving end of. I always also remember the layers of sabotage I experienced in the workplace as a Black woman principal in New Orleans at the hand of both white fragility and Black co-conspirators. The very things I was silenced for doing and enacting back then are the *very* same things I'm highly sought after to teach teachers, school leaders, and systems, including school systems in which some of those same actors who were involved in my unjust termination are present within.

Some people think of this, as I did too earlier on, as the epitome of how things come full circle. However, I think now about how our children and schools suffer and pay for the choices that adults make at the end of the day, so when I read this snippet of MPS's case study it broke my heart but didn't surprise me. There are many adults who show up to work every day to serve children with the purest of hearts but have to deal with so much turmoil, unrest, disrespect, offense, lack of psychological safety, lack of emotional safety, and more.

Reflections on my own experience should make us all consider the following:

- The extent to which schools and organizations of all kinds within the education sector identify dominant culture—in my case, white dominant culture—as affecting the ability of staff members—in my case staff of color—to effectively participate, contribute, or be accepted in the workplace
- The extent to which staff members of color (or other groups if you were to interchange race with gender, sexuality, language, etc.) feel as though they can be their full authentic selves within a school or system
- The extent to which staff members of color feel silenced, punished, or mistreated (e.g., looked over for promotion), particularly as a result of being their full authentic selves; in my case, being "too Black" in championing practices that centered our students' Black heritage and communities' lived experiences
- The extent to which schools normalize self-care (for our kids and for adults, and at minimum even acknowledging what has taken place) especially when a traumatic event has happened or when there is a triggering environment that disproportionately and directly affects communities of color
- The extent to which schools or systems regularly acknowledge racial events by creating space for staff members to process collectively or individually as they need to and understanding that racially motivated incidents often affect people of color differently than white people/staff members

Let's check out the actions MPS chose to enact as a result of these findings:

Human Resources EDIA Proposal
Overview
Based on the findings of the EDIA process, the EDIA Committee provided MPS with feedback on ways to address the challenges identified. Human Resources (HR) and Accountability, Research, and Equity (ARE) worked collaboratively to develop an initial action plan based on the report and the Committee feedback. This initial plan includes many technical solutions, but the goal is that it will lead to the adaptive changes in culture that are needed for long term success in making MPS a welcoming environment for our staff of color. We will begin with partial implementation in SY19 with full implementation in SY20. HR and ARE presented this proposed plan to the EDIA Committee and the committee's additional feedback is embedded within.

Ongoing HR Commitments
Continue to develop pipelines and career trajectories for critical and hard-to-staff positions across the District, including our Special Education Residency program
    Centralize and enhance onboarding to attract, excite and retain strong staff
    Design recruitment and retention training for leaders
    Create and activate recruitment networks and partnerships with our schools and communities
    Increasing exit reflection session participation to identify ways we can better support staff

Proposed MPS HR & Department Efforts Human Resources
Hiring and Recruitment
    Add an additional Recruitment and Retention Coordinator to engage deeply and authentically with our broad MPS community, and provide feedback from community stakeholders to HR on ways that we can continually improve.
    Expand our recruitment budget to more explicitly emphasize active, community-focused, and out of state recruitment efforts.
    Deepen and expand the extent to which we train hiring managers and interview teams on implicit bias in the hiring process, in order to ensure that all candidates are being treated fairly and consistently, and helping to ensure that we can continue to diversify our workforce.
    Reframe our annual higher education partnership event to showcase and amplify voices of teachers of color, to help our preparation partners better understand and prepare candidates for the authentic experiences of educators of color in MPS.
    Investigate how new rules with the Professional Educator Licensing and Standards Board (PELSB) regarding including teachers of color as part of the definition of

"hard-to-fill" licensure areas can support our broader effort to increase the diversity of our new teacher hires.

Articulate how SOEI and SOESL (performance management rubrics for teachers and principals) indicators demonstrate equitable practices in order to embed and crosswalk the language of equity into how we talk about, give feedback around, and measure effective practice.

Human Resources: Support and Retention

Hire a Mediator dedicated fully to helping employees resolve issues that are affecting their job satisfaction without having these issues rise to the level of formal Human Resources or Equal Opportunity Office processes. This new role would create a safe space for employees to share their thoughts, provide a structure for mediation between employees, and help maintain a positive staff culture across the district.

Offer in-person feedback and reflection sessions to all interested teachers of color who are leaving the district in order to gain critical insight into the reasons that we are losing talented staff.

Increase levels of mentorship support for teachers of color in MPS. This could take the form of hiring additional PAR mentors for supporting early-career teachers, but could also represent new or innovative models for ongoing mentorship support for teachers of color.

Emphasize the elimination of disparities as an explicit focus in contract negotiations, particularly with our teacher's contract. Specifically, the EDIA Committee identified areas such as the internal hiring process and seniority-based layoffs as potential places for improvement.

Departments of Academics & Accountability, Research, and Equity

Ensure all MPS leadership complete the IDI Assessment and engage in ongoing equity professional development (Cabinet, Executive Directors, Directors, Principals, APs).

Add additional equity coaches to assist school leaders in supporting positive and inclusive climate.

Train principals on EDIA process and create tools for small-scale, school-based EDIA processes. Doing so will allow the effects and impacts of the EDIA process to unfold at the site level.

Examine and leverage the new district calendar, which presents new opportunities to provide additional professional development around equity to teachers at the beginning of each school year.

Support affinity groups for teachers of color and provide avenues to access system leaders and decision makers.

Review current staff and student survey data (from the 5E, spring survey, and others), and triangulate findings with HR data to inform improvements to school culture and climate by understanding both the student and staff experience with school environments across the district.

Timeline and Accountability
Partial implementation of the plan will begin this school year, with additional invest-
ments and implementation for SY20. HR and ARE will meet with the EDIA commit-
tee quarterly to provide updates on implementation and gather feedback to inform
and modify the plan.

REFLECTION QUESTION

What do you notice in the Minneapolis Public Schools artifacts? What is most pronounced?

GUIDING QUESTIONS

Here are questions educational leaders can use to understand the state of DEI within HR, as well as to understand the state of staff culture and climate:

- Does your school, district, network, nonprofit, or company have a DEI framework or plan in place?
- Does your school, district, network, nonprofit, or company's DEI framework and/or plan have clear actions, timelines, and people responsible for each action?
- Does your school, district, network, nonprofit, or company's DEI framework and/or plan have clear indicators of progress (KPIs, or key performance indicators)?
- Does your school, district, network, nonprofit, or company's DEI framework and/or plan have clear processes for monitoring and evaluation?
- If you have developed, or are developing, a written DEI plan, who was involved in its development?

- To what extent are cultural competency knowledge, skills, and practices incorporated into performance objectives (such as job descriptions and work plans) and appraisals/evaluations for staff members within your school, district, network, nonprofit, or company?
- Do performance appraisals/evaluations include progress on explicit DEI competencies or goals?
- Are there effective formal and informal procedures for staff members regarding race-related complaints?
- Are there effective formal and informal procedures for staff members regarding gender-related complaints?
- Are there effective formal and informal procedures for staff members regarding sexuality/sexual orientation–related complaints?
- Are DEI trainings voluntary or mandatory within your school, district, network, nonprofit, or company?
- Within your school, district, network, nonprofit, or company, who is expected to oversee DEI initiatives as a whole?
- Are there visible signs or any form of external communication of your school, district, network, nonprofit, or company's commitment to DEI?
- Does your school, district, network, nonprofit, or company encourage or support difficult conversations about race, or do we shy away from doing so?
- Does your school, district, network, nonprofit, or company encourage or support difficult conversations about gender and sexuality, or do you all shy away from doing so?
- Does your school, district, network, nonprofit, or company encourage or support difficult conversations about class and socioeconomic status, or do you all shy away from doing so?
- Does your school, district, network, nonprofit, or company encourage or support difficult conversations about any form of social injustice, harm, or oppression, or do you all shy away from doing so?
- What practices or structures does your school, district, network, nonprofit, or company have in place to support employees of color (e.g., mentoring, employee support groups, comprehensive orientations)?
- Are there supports for employees of color to move into positions with low diversity?
- What practices or structures does your school, district, network, nonprofit, or company have in place to support LGBTQIA+ employees (e.g., employee support groups)?
- What practices or structures does your school, district, network, nonprofit, or company have in place to support employees with mental health challenges?
- How does your school, district, network, nonprofit, or company market, brand and/or message your equity initiatives?

- How is your school, district, network, nonprofit, or company's internal culture of inclusion and equity communicated? Practices may include noticing barriers to participation, planning that incorporates participation supports, public appreciation of "out loud" interrupting or naming of inequities, and encouragement when difficult topics are surfaced.
- What is the racial/ethnic composition of each of the varying staff member roles/types within your school, district, network, nonprofit, or company?
- What traits and qualities are valued with each varying staff member role/position within your organization or team? Who determines the traits and qualities that are prioritized and how they are defined (what they look like)? To what extent are the traits and qualities white dominant or reflective of other dominant groups in ways that create very real barriers for those who are not members of a dominant group?
- Where are your school, district, network, nonprofit, or company's job postings placed?
- What target audience accesses each particular avenue of advertisement?
- What target audience is at an advantage within promotion of the job vacancies using the platform your school, district, network, nonprofit, or company has chosen?
- Who is at a disadvantage? How do we mitigate or address any particular discrepancies within your school, district, network, nonprofit, or company's recruitment processes?
- To what extent does the leadership team ensure that the organization or team engages in exhaustive approaches to recruit and retain diverse talent across a variety of roles?
- To what extent is there preferential treatment within which prospective candidates matriculate through the interview process?
- If the position will work with racially, ethnically, and socioeconomically diverse communities, to what extent does your organization or team vet for these qualities:

  - Experience working directly with persons from diverse racial, ethnic, and socioeconomic backgrounds
  - Ability to speak a second language or ability to speak ____ language (if the position will be working with a particular community)
  - Views, perspectives, and beliefs regarding race, class, and other areas of social identity

- Who comprises your school, district, network, nonprofit, or company's hiring committee?
- To what extent is there racial diversity on your interview review panel? Is there a balanced representation of people of color at each stage of the interview process? Is there required bias training for hiring committee members?
- To what extent has the organization or team created an environment that normalizes learning about institutional bias and racism, including self-reflection about one's relationship to these systems?
- To what extent is there a formal or informal check-in regularly within your school, district, network, nonprofit, or company examining the experiences of marginalized staff members within the workplace? If so, how often? If so, who does so? If so, how is that information used?
- To what extent do members of marginalized groups feel as though they have what they need to be successful within your school, district, network, nonprofit, or company?

- To what extent are there transparent and effective communication and processes used to evaluate staff members?
- Does your organization or team provide all staff members with individual professional growth plans?
- What is the rate at which staff members of color (and other groups) stay within your organization or team?
- How much are employees of color (and other groups) paid in comparison to white counterparts in similar positions within your school, district, nonprofit, or company?
- How frequently do staff members of color within our organization or team get promoted? How long does it take to get a career advancement opportunity?
- In light of any recruitment, hiring, and retention concerns, has our organization or team created concrete strategies and goals to address them? What has been accomplished so far? If it isn't successful, have we analyzed why not? Do efforts specifically address institutional racism and bias?
- To what extent does the organization or team promote a narrow portrait of what leader competency looks like/sounds like/feels like (e.g., looking for "joy" within adults in a monolithic way)? Are our portraits of leader excellence inclusive?
- To what extent do white staff members at our organization or team comfortably own possession of white privilege? To what extent is there denial of white privilege?
- To what extent does our organization or team promote the idea of being "colorblind" in our approach and engagement among colleagues?
- To what extent does your school, district, network, nonprofit, or company provide ongoing learning opportunities, such as workshops, reading groups, lectures, training modules, and other forms of adult learning that explore topics designed to equip staff members with greater cultural awareness, knowledge, skills, and practices?
- Has your school, district, network, nonprofit, or company formalized staff member affinity groups, especially to support community members from marginalized groups?

REFLECTION QUESTIONS

Which guiding questions capture your attention the most as you consider HR within your school, system, nonprofit, or organization, and why?

Which guiding question represents a growth area for you and/or your school, district, nonprofit, or company?

Which guiding question represents an area of strength for you and/or your school, district, nonprofit, or company?

SAMPLE NEXT STEPS

Here are sample actions school and district leaders may take:

- As a school, network, district, nonprofit, or company, create a cultural competency domain of your performance evaluation system, so that staff members also receive formal feedback on the ways in which they live out or demonstrate cultural competency.
- As a school, network, district, nonprofit, or company, incorporate targeted DEI questions within your interviewing and hiring process for all candidates, as well as non-negotiable responses that signify red flags.
- As a school, network, district, nonprofit, or company, incorporate a formal feedback system and process that allows for expression of racial (or other social identity-based) grievances.
- As a school, network, district, nonprofit, or company, adopt or create a staff culture/climate survey that also incorporates racial equity question stems in order to regularly collect racial equity data, analyze it, and adjust course (be it celebrating positives or addressing negative findings).

- As a school, network, district, nonprofit, or company, post and share job openings within these arenas:

  - Community newspapers, as well as news websites run by communities of color, particularly websites dedicated to educators and educational leaders from marginalized communities
  - Multicultural centers or cultural studies departments at local colleges and universities in your city, state, or region of the United States
  - Four-year colleges and universities that center serving historically marginalized groups.
  - Community colleges and schools with a large number of students of color, either graduate or undergrad, alumni associations, or current job boards or students from other marginalized communities
  - Job boards, websites, social media accounts, and in-person job or community events hosted by organizations that serve communities of color, particularly educators or educational leaders of color or other marginalized groups
  - Professional associations (e.g., National Association of Black School Educators), affinity groups within professional associations, and networks of professionals of color or other marginalized communities
  - Organizational partners that represent and serve communities of color, particularly educators of color or other marginalized groups
  - Affinity or employee resource groups

7

Teaching and Learning (Instruction)

This domain is by far one of the most important aspects of operationalizing DEI that educators can take active steps toward actualizing. High-quality instruction drives the success of student outcomes in a variety of different ways. Conversely, the lack of high-quality instruction can serve as a barrier to the overall growth and progression of students outcomes within a school, system, or network. Whether a school system serves racially, linguistically, or even socioeconomically diverse students, centering DEI within teaching and learning is important. There are so many different types of learners within our classrooms and schools. As a reminder, our schools—be they public or private—serve students who represent a wide variety of people:

- **Various racial and ethnic groups.**
- Examples include but are not limited to mindfulness of Black, Latino, Asian-American, Pacific Islander, Indigenous, and more racial and ethnic communities of students.
- **Varying genders.**
- Examples include but are not limited to males (young men and boys), females (young women and girls), cisgendered, gender fluid, gender nonconforming, and other gender categories of students.
- **Different neurodiversity backgrounds and needs.**
- Examples of neurodivergence include but are not limited to students with autism, attention deficit/hyperactivity disorder (ADHD), dyslexia, dysgraphia, and more
- **Different socioeconomic or financial backgrounds.**
- Examples include but are not limited to students from low-income backgrounds, which is also divided between those that simply draw from low or lower wages or salaries versus individuals who live extremely below the poverty line. Diversity within socioeconomic background also includes students from middle-class or -income backgrounds, which isn't a monolithic group either similar to the aforementioned example of individuals—especially students—of lower income background.
- **Different sexualities or sexual orientations.**
- Examples include but are not limited to individuals who are heterosexual, bisexual, asexual, pansexual, and other sexual orientations our students, we ourselves, our colleagues, families, and other stakeholders identify as.

- **Different family backgrounds.**
- Examples include but are not limited to grandparent-led households, households of same-sex marriages so for students this might translate to but not be limited to two moms or two dads being present at home; foster families, adopted families, and more.

The implications for what and how teachers teach are vast and wide. So, when we think of DEI within teaching and learning, we must think about the following:

- Our academic standards
- The curriculum we use
- Our selection of text
- Academic goal setting
- Long-term and unit planning
- Lesson planning
- Lesson delivery or execution
- Assessments
- Data analysis and planning

When we consider the standards we drive toward, particularly if you are a key decision- or policy maker at the state level, you must consider the extent to which your standards are inclusive or not. A very easy example of this is consideration of your history standard. What history are you teaching? Is it accurate? Whose stories, heritages, and histories are you elevating and amplifying? Whose stories, heritages, and histories are you hiding, not speaking to, or ignoring? Is there any heritage, community, or history you're altering, limiting, or watering down?

When you consider the curriculum your school, network, or district uses, you must consider who is being represented within it, how they're being represented, what messages you are sending about varying groups through your curricular choice, and how the curriculum will serve different profiles of learners. Although these are just two examples of considerations, next you'll see practical recommendations for ways to center and advance DEI within the classroom.

SAMPLE FRAMEWORKS

Here, you'll find snippets of a great DEI framework for teachers, teacher mentors, instructional coaches, or anyone supporting teachers in the classroom who truly wants to dive deeper in being more intentional within their own DEI practices.

The following is an excerpt from the New York State Education Department (NYSED)'s "Culturally Responsive-Sustaining Education Framework":

TEACHERS
Competency: Fostering High Expectations and Rigorous Instruction

Have high expectations and deliver rigorous instruction for all students regardless of identity markers, including race, gender, sexual orientation, language, ability, and economic background.

Reflect on your own implicit bias, how that bias might impact your expectations for student achievement or the decisions you make in the classroom, and the steps you can take to address your biases and their impact on students.

Strive to be culturally sustaining by centering the identities of all students in classroom instruction, encouraging cultural pluralism rather than asking students to minimize their identities in order to be successful.

Provide parents with information about what their child is expected to learn, know, and do at his/her grade level and ways to reinforce concepts at home (e.g., using the home language; reading with, or monitoring, independent reading).

Promote alternative achievement metrics that also support academics (e.g., demonstrating growth, leadership, character development, Social Emotional Learning competencies, or school values).

Invite families and community members to speak or read in the classroom as a means to teach about topics that are culturally specific and aligned to the classroom curriculum and/or content area.

Provide opportunities for students to critically examine topics of power and privilege. These can be planned project-based learning initiatives, instructional activities embedded into the curriculum, or discussion protocols used in response to inequity that occurs in the school and/or classroom.

Incorporate current events, even if they are controversial, into instruction. Utilize tools (prompting discussion questions, Socratic seminar, conversation protocols) that encourage students to engage with difficult topics (power, privilege, access, inequity) constructively.

Be responsive to students' experiences by providing them with a space to process current events.

Help students identify their different learning styles in both classwork and homework and incorporate instructional strategies and assignments that are responsive to those learning styles.

Provide students with opportunities to present to their peers through project-based or stations-based learning to leverage student experience and expertise. Co-create explicit classroom expectations that meet the needs of all students.

Competency: Identifying Inclusive Curriculum and Assessment

Feature and highlight resources written and developed by traditionally marginalized voices that offer diverse perspectives on race, culture, language, gender, sexual identity, ability, religion, nationality, migrant/refugee status, socioeconomic status, housing status, and other identities traditionally silenced or omitted from curriculum.

Play a role in helping schools to understand and align curriculum to the variety of histories, languages and experiences that reflect the diversity of the State population.

Pair traditional curricular content with digital and other media platforms that provide current and relevant context from youth culture.

Provide homework, projects, and other classroom materials in multiple languages.

Provide regular opportunities for social emotional learning strategies within lessons and as discrete learning activities.

Utilize student data points and assessment measures that reflect learning spaces, modalities, and demonstration of proficiency that go beyond metrics traditionally associated with standardized testing.

Engage students in youth participatory action research that empowers youth to be agents of positive change in their community.

Connect instructional content with the daily lives of students by using culturally specific examples (e.g., music, movies, text) that tap into their existing interests, knowledge, and youth culture.

Take field trips to community-learning sites, such as museums, parks, cultural centers, neighborhood recreational centers, and community centers, to foster students' cultural understanding and connection to the surrounding community.

Incorporate cooperative learning activities to encourage understanding of diverse perspectives; support students in working cooperatively toward goals; and highlight students' unique strengths in the group (e.g., public speaking, note-taking, writing, drawing, etc.).

Support students in creating and running student-led initiatives.

Building on this framework, the next framework is an excerpt from Learning for Justice (formerly Teaching Tolerance)'s "Best Practices for Serving English Language Learners" guide, which was published in 2017.

Culturally Responsive ELL Instruction

Create a responsive room environment. A classroom should reflect the identities of the children who learn there. Think about the posters, flags, images, and people featured on your classroom walls. Do all your ELL students see themselves in the decor?

Make the curriculum relevant. Embed stories, readings, and perspectives that focus on history, immigration, and community into the units you teach. This will create opportunities to bring personal stories to the classroom and show students that their lives are a part of the United States' long history with changing borders and movements of people.

Use a variety of teaching modalities. Movement, call-and-response, claps, stomps, chants, and cheers are all ways to get—and keep—the attention of students who may not understand every word. These approaches also offer opportunities to make memorable connections to the curriculum. Graphic organizers, sentence stems, visual thinking strategies, and journals are just a few instructional strategies educators can incorporate to make the curriculum more accessible and less intimidating to ELL students.

Familiarize yourself with cultural norms. Respect looks different in different parts of the world. Don't make assumptions about ELL students without seeking out some information about the messages their behavior may be sending.

Get to know your students' contextual skills and educational backgrounds. Educational structures and norms vary from country to country. Making assumptions— for example that students are used to interacting with printed materials—can impede your instructional relationship. Similarly, informally assessing kids for skills such as using scissors, writing on lined paper, writing the date, or using art supplies can save students from embarrassment in front of teachers and peers.

Distinguish between academic English and conversational/home English. Some ELL students speak conversational English at home but are less familiar with academic English. Rather than seeing this as a deficit and continually correcting students' use of their home language, show them similarities and differences, creating bridges between home and academic English. As a general rule, it takes 5 to 7 years to become proficient in conversational English and 7 to 11 years to reach proficiency in academic English. It is also important to note that, although some students may speak conversational English well, they may still need ELL services to help them with academic English skills.

Honor your students' first languages. If you know a student is literate in another language, find ways to bring it into the classroom and celebrate its use at home and at school.

Limit pull-out instruction time. Pulling ELL students out of class for separate instruction limits contact time with peers. ELL students who spend a significant amount of time outside of the classroom are put at a disadvantage for forming new friendships and learning new skills.

Level the playing field. Provide leveled reading material in a student's native language, and be sure to give ELL students the same curriculum that everyone else is using. ELL students may need additional scaffolding or alternative texts, but everyone should be given access to the same essential questions, learning targets, and enduring understandings.

Provide all students the opportunity to showcase their talents and cultures through assignments such as a community art showcase or a photo essay exhibit. Provide texts that serve as mirrors to your ELL students' lived experiences and cultures and as windows for their peers.

Model being a language learner. Allow ELL students to teach you and other students about their languages and cultures. Apply for a grant that will fund language classes for school staff. Learn some phrases in your students' native languages and then use them.

Go beyond the classroom. Provide opportunities for ELL and non-ELL students to interact and work together outside of the classroom. Working alongside their peers helps ELL students gain a sense of accomplishment and take pride in knowing that they have something to contribute.

REFLECTION QUESTIONS

Which of the previous recommendations stand out to you the most, and why?

Are there recommendations that speak to the work you are already engaged in? If so, is this an area of strength for you or your school?

Are there recommendations above that speak to areas for growth for you or your school community?

ADDITIONAL TOOLS

Here are additional sample frameworks for different aspects of diversity—such as language, exceptionalities, etc.—for your review:

■ Teaching Tolerance's "Best Practices for Serving English Language Learners And Their Families"

- The National Association of Special Education Teachers' "Effective Teaching Strategies for Students with LD" reports
- The National Center for Culturally Responsive Education Systems' "Equity in Special Education: A School Self-Assessment Guide for Culturally Responsive Practice" guide
- New America's "Culturally Responsive Teaching: A Reflection Guide"
- UCLA's "Reimagining Migration: Culturally Responsive Teaching Checklist"
- Perspective of a Diverse America's & Teaching Tolerance's "Critical Practices for Anti-Bias Education" guide
- Hanover Research's "Best Practices for Trauma-Informed Instruction"

GUIDING QUESTIONS

Now that you've seen some examples of how to intentionally integrate and center DEI within the classroom and will be reviewing the additional recommended resources, let's look at what central or guiding questions your organization should be asking yourselves formally or informally within this domain of teaching and learning.

I propose that you ask yourselves the following:

- To what extent have you as a teacher created a shared vision for academic success/excellence with a variety of perspectives/stakeholders' input in mind? If so, with whom did we construct our vision?
- To what extent is your school/network/district or your own articulation and definition of what success looks like narrow and aligned to an internalized belief that students' proximity to whiteness or assimilation within white dominant culture and/or norms define success in life?
- To what extent does your school, network, district, nonprofit, or company disaggregate academic data across racial lines? Socioeconomic lines? Gender lines? Linguistic lines?
- As it relates to goal setting, does your school, network, district, nonprofit, or company establish targets and indicators of success that will answer the question, Are we adequately meeting the needs of all student groups?
- Do your school, network, district, nonprofit, or company's instructional plans incorporate tiered and scaffolded supports for all learners?
- Does your school, network, district, nonprofit, or company pair traditional curricular content with digital and other media platforms that provide current and relevant context from youth culture?
- As it relates to academic performance, to what extent does your school, network, district, nonprofit, or company have low expectations for any particular group of students?
- As it relates to race, to what extent are your school, network, district, nonprofit, or company's expectations for students of color different than those for their white counterparts?

- Would the expectations that your school, network, district, nonprofit, or company hold for students be considered high expectations in a different school setting (e.g., white, affluent, etc.)?
- Within distance learning, does your school, network, district, nonprofit, or company provide structured instructional time to meet the needs of students with varying levels of access to the internet and technology?
- Does your school, network, district, nonprofit, or company use varied strategies for providing at-home learning support?
- Does your school, network, district, nonprofit, or company formally assess instructional materials for racial or other forms of bias? If so, when/how often?
- Who determines whether instructional materials are appropriate or not, and are they adequately knowledgeable or equipped to do so?
- To what extent are your school, network, district, nonprofit, or company's curriculum and instructional materials Eurocentric or white dominant in nature?
- Do you align curriculum to the variety of histories, languages, and experiences that reflect the diversity of your city/state/our country?
- Does the curriculum/instructional material(s) your school, network, district, nonprofit, or company uses reflect values of DEI? To what extent are they culturally affirming?
- Does your school, network, district, nonprofit, or company incorporate use of measurable goals to monitor progress that narrow gaps between the least and most advantaged students?
- Does your school, network, district, nonprofit, or company specify provisions for students with disabilities and students in need of specialized instruction, related services, or other supports?
- Does your school, network, district, nonprofit, or company specify supports and instructional strategies to meet the needs of English learners?
- Does your school, network, district, nonprofit, or company provide access to translated instructional materials or translation services for non-English-speaking caregivers to support student learning?
- Does your school, network, district, nonprofit, or company have explicit means of ensuring high-quality and differentiated instruction for students previously and currently enrolled in alternative settings (i.e., state operated programs, specialty programs, alternative schools, etc.)?
- To what extent does your school, network, district, nonprofit, or company build all staff members' capacity to cultivate critical consciousness and transform their curriculum/instructional plans in ways that are inclusive? This requires ongoing curriculum transformation efforts (e.g., decolonization, etc.) and staff development resources.
- To what extent does your school, network, district, nonprofit, or company provide instructional content that does the following:
  - Celebrates students' culture/heritage/background in a seamless and ongoing manner?
  - Perpetuates any form of classism or colorism?
  - Perpetuates any white supremacy in provision of limited and/or inaccurate information, particularly within history, the sciences, and so on?

- Aligns to or with the principles of culturally responsive pedagogy as outlined within academic research (e.g., Gloria Ladson Billings, Paul Gorski, Geneva Gay, etc.)?

- Is culturally relevant pedagogy formally assessed with observation and feedback cycles for all teachers?
- To what extent does the following occur at your school:
    - Teachers encourage students to attend college (four-year universities, two-year junior colleges, etc.)?
    - Teachers voice college as the singular pathway to success?
    - Teachers encourage students to pursue a trade or other forms of nontraditional career pathways?
    - Students of color, especially Black students, excused and allowed to disengage from academic work?
    - Teachers assign challenging student work tasks/assignments?
    - Black and Brown students encouraged to take advanced classes?
    - Black and Brown students placed within remedial classes?
    - Black and Brown students overly referred to/placed in special education courses?

- Does your school, network, district, nonprofit, or company establish opportunities for subject-level and grade-level committees that involve community-based or parental input, and include cultural knowledge throughout the curriculum?
- As it relates to racial equity, to what degree are Black and Brown staff members recognized and properly credited for their work and contributions?
- As it relates to gender equity, to what degree are women and other marginalized genders recognized and properly credited for their work and contributions?
- Does your school, network, district, nonprofit, or company actively create space to reflect on implicit bias, how that bias might affect your expectations for student achievement or the decisions you made in classrooms, and the steps you all can take to address your biases and their impact on students?
- Does your school, network, district, nonprofit, or company actively strive to be culturally sustaining by centering the identities of all students in classroom instruction, encouraging cultural pluralism rather than asking students to minimize their identities in order to be successful?
- Does your school, network, district, nonprofit, or company consistently provide parents with information about what their child is expected to learn, know, and do at his/her grade level and ways to reinforce concepts at home (e.g., using the home language, reading with, or monitoring, independent reading)?
- As a school, network, district, nonprofit, or company, do you promote alternative achievement metrics that also support academics (e.g., demonstrating growth, leadership, character development, social emotional learning competencies, or school values)?
- As a school, network, district, nonprofit, or company, do you invite families and community members to speak, read, or engage in the classroom, as a means to teach about topics that are culturally specific and aligned to the classroom curriculum and/or content area?

- As a school, network, district, nonprofit, or company, do you provide opportunities for students to critically examine topics of power and privilege? These can be planned project-based learning initiatives, instructional activities embedded into the curriculum, or discussion protocols used in response to inequity that occurs in the school and/or classroom.
- As a school, network, district, nonprofit, or company, do you consistently incorporate current events, even if they are controversial, into instruction? This can include using tools (prompting discussion questions, Socratic seminar, conversation protocols) that encourage students to engage with difficult topics (power, privilege, access, inequity) constructively.
- Particularly when moments of racial unrest occur, as a school, network, district, nonprofit, or company, are you responsive to students' experiences by providing them with a space to process current events?
- Does your school, network, district, nonprofit, or company help students identify their different learning styles in both classwork and homework and incorporate instructional strategies and assignments that are responsive to those learning styles?
- Does your school, network, district, nonprofit, or company provide students with opportunities to present to their peers through project-based or stations-based learning to leverage student experience and expertise?
- Does your school, network, or district, cocreate explicit classroom expectations that meet the needs of all students?
- When and how often do you feature and highlight resources written and developed by traditionally marginalized voices that offer diverse perspectives on race, culture, language, gender, sexual identity, ability, religion, nationality, migrant/refugee status, socioeconomic status, housing status, and other identities traditionally silenced or omitted from curriculum?
- As a school, network, or district, to what extent do we provide homework, projects, and other classroom materials in multiple languages?
- As a school, network, or district, to what extent do we provide regular opportunities for social emotional learning strategies within lessons and as discrete learning activities?
- As a school, network, or district, to what extent do we use student data points and assessment measures that reflect learning spaces, modalities, and demonstration of proficiency that go beyond metrics traditionally associated with standardized testing?
- As a school, network, district, nonprofit, or company, to what extent do we engage students in youth participatory action research that empowers youth to be agents of positive change in their community?
- As a school, network, or district, to what extent do we take field trips to community-learning sites, such as museums, parks, cultural centers, neighborhood recreational centers, and community centers, to foster students' cultural understanding and connection to the surrounding community?

- As a school, network, or district, to what extent do we incorporate cooperative learning activities to encourage understanding of diverse perspectives; support students in working cooperatively toward goals; and highlight students' unique strengths in the group (e.g., public speaking, note-taking, writing, drawing, etc.)?

Given the previous questions, let's think about how this applies to you.

REFLECTION QUESTIONS

As you consider your own school and classroom instruction across your campus, which guiding questions capture your attention the most and why?

Which guiding question represents a growth area for you and/or your school?

Which guiding question represents an area of strength for you and/or your school?

SAMPLE NEXT STEPS

Here are sample actions principals, instructional leadership teams, and district leaders may take in this area of operationalizing DEI:

- As a school, network, or district, strategize instructional methods to disrupt any disparities in student success outcomes that exist across lines of difference, highlighting and sharing best practices from the field.
- As a school, network, or district, incorporate adaptive learning methods that encourage differentiation, exploration, and curiosity as opposed to scripted, one-size-fits-all instructional programs.
- As a school, network, or district, partner with experts in the field (i.e., professional learning organizations, higher education, consultants) to identify research-based, instructional strategies that are most effective in advancing student academic success.
- As a school, network, or district, use tools to identify and recognize instructional methods that high-performing, culturally responsive–sustaining teachers are using across content areas.
- As a school, network, or district, facilitate structures for teacher collaboration across school and district teams, that is, peer observations, school visits, purposeful partnerships, mentor teachers, and so on.

8

Student Culture and Climate

As you think about student culture and climate, here are factors I believe are vital (or vitally important) for you to consider:

- Student–teacher relationships
- Student–student relationships
- Administrator–student relationships
- Artifacts (e.g., student handbook)
- Behavior rules, expectations, and policies
- Consequences
- Rewards and incentives
- Student programming (e.g., clubs, events, etc.)
- Physical environment
- Traditions and customs
- Core values, mindsets, and beliefs
- Language

I'd also like us to take a moment to think about one reality and phenomenon so many students face across varying lines of difference: trauma. There are different types and levels of trauma, for example, racial trauma, and our children are experiencing trauma from so many different sources. I think about what happens inside school spaces and outside as well. Sometimes it's community violence or gun violence they've been a witness to, and because of its high volume, they've even become numb to it at an early age and desensitized to the value of human life. Sometimes it's on the receiving end of a parent or grandparent or family member not necessarily providing the love, care, time, attention, or emotional support needed to affirm how they feel or provide the messages that they need to hear to develop a positive sense of self-identity.

There are also a lot of sociocultural and political events occurring within educational landscapes across the country that our kids watch on TV. And because social media is widely accessible—our children have Snapchat accounts, they have Facebook accounts, Instagram, and so on—they're being exposed to a lot of information, much of which is unfiltered.

I think about the internal experience in schools by the way in which our children are talked to and the way in which they are addressed. Children who often, in a very unspoken way, are asking for help. I think about how often children may be misdiagnosed when they display a behavior or action, but we're not necessarily asking the question, "What is the actual root cause and how are we creating solutions that address what this particular child actually needs underneath the behavior that we see manifested?" I also think about the bullying that can happen in the school context and outside of the school context.

For all of these reasons, I think about the relationship between the environment and children's psyches. Facilities matter. Having worked within a school facility that had limited windows and no grass for children to play on, I think about what it means to be in a prison-like building for eight hours straight, asked to carry a heavy cognitive lift on doing academic tasks, but not given enough time to play, exercise, just be a kid. I think of a lot of ways that children are facing different traumatic experiences and are not necessarily given the space to voice them. Even if they don't have the technical language to describe what it is that they're feeling, it's important to create space for them to just talk, to name their concerns, the things that are stressing them out, and dream.

I can think of a young girl who really manifested a lot of intense, aggressive behaviors, in particular in moments in which she might not have gotten the outcome that she wanted from adults or from a peer. She would scream. She would yell. She would kick. She would run. As a school community, myself included, we gave so much attention to this young girl in those behavioral moments and in a lot of other ways, but the follow-up and follow-through of maintaining this support dropped. We operated in a very reactive way to support this young girl instead of a proactive way. That sends a message to a child who will think, "I got so much attention doing that, so I know what to do to get what I want." Instead of concentrating on her behavior in the here and now, we should have given her an opportunity for her voice to enter into the process so that we better understood what her true needs were.

We need to put children first in the conversation. Yet other folks experience our educational system as well: parents, educators, and other stakeholders to education. I think a lot about preparation for teachers and educators, in general, but also for other staff members, such as principals and school social workers. There's room and space for our educators to be trained on not only what trauma-informed practices are but also the *why* and the *how*. What are the different types of trauma? What does it look like? And, really, it helps adults navigate through their own traumatic experience because it's going to be hard for me to lead you to a place that I also haven't navigated. We need to create spaces for adults as practitioners to process their own experiences and how those experiences show up in the way they speak, the decisions they make, how they design their classroom, and the rules and expectations they set for kids. We can provide space for a certain degree of healing for those adults. That coupled with giving them the technical tools and the language and strategies and methods to really operate in a more trauma-informed way is important because we have to balance the work of the head and the heart. By providing this support we are really compelling a different way of thinking. We're shifting beliefs and convictions, along with providing actual tools through professional development and adult learning opportunities.

Another avenue to leverage in your path of centering and advancing DEI is the wisdom, strength, and collective knowledge of our communities. Our communities are rich with so many assets that we don't exhaustively leverage in schools and systems. Often when the word *assets* is used, the train of thinking is financial, specifically as it relates to funding and development. Yet there's so much that local churches, nonprofits, elders, and communities, in addition to numerous other people and stakeholders, can provide to help create a holistic, vibrant community that our children deserve. A lot of the work on systems and schools is also about creating much more intentional, strategic, and deep community partnerships, because a lot of the partnerships we have are very transactional, very one and done. This might look like creating authentic rapport and meaningful partnership with organizations such as your city's local chapter of 100 Black Men, local Black fraternities and sororities, your city's local chapter of The Urban League, and even local community support organizations.

Ultimately, what happens when we give our children the opportunity to share their perspective? What types of stories would they tell? What would their parents, guardians, and families say? When we bring everyone together, it elevates our understanding of the many facets of trauma so we don't rely on a single archetype for a traumatic experience. Rather, we can recognize all the micro and the macro ways in which trauma can occur every single day. That type of opportunity just makes all of us far more conscious of and reflective on situations we've experienced in our own lifetime, but also highlights ways in which we unintentionally perpetuate the very same things that we profess to and have conviction to fight. Additionally, there's an opportunity for policy to be shaped and crafted to institutionalize the learning from this type of professional development for educators, increased parental voices, and increased community input. Without broader input, there's not necessarily the incentive for systems to make others' voices a priority in evaluating and crafting policy. And if family and community engagement are not being evaluated, and if there are not explicit asks and requirements, or, for some folks, dollars connected to the family and community engagement nor student culture and climate efforts a school seeks to enact, people often don't do it or follow through with upholding high-quality programming for students, families, and their community stakeholders.

SAMPLE FRAMEWORK

Dr. Maya Angelou once said, "People may forget what you say, people may forget what you do, but people will never forget the way you made them feel." For the millions of students served across our country, there are a plethora of beliefs, practices, and policies that are vital to discover in order to ensure that our schools and districts are safe and transformational environments for children. This not only pertains to their physical safety from harm but also includes the psychological and emotional safety of all children. To be clear, being physically safe does not mean that you're automatically also mentally and emotionally okay and safe within the walls of a classroom or school. One framework I encourage you to check out is the National Center on Safe Supportive Learning Environments' framework, "Positive School Climate."

The following is an excerpt from the New York State Education Department (NYSED)'s "Culturally Responsive-Sustaining Education Framework" pertaining to classroom culture:

Teacher Version: Creating a Welcoming and Affirming Environment

- *Assess the physical environment of the classroom and school to determine whether a variety of diverse cultures, languages, orientations, and identities are reflected, represented, and valued. Promote a variety of perspectives that represent the diversity of the state of New York beyond designated icons, historical figures, months, and holidays.*
- *Build rapport and develop positive relationships with students, and their families, by learning about their interests and inviting them to share their opinions and concerns. Find opportunities to address and incorporate their opinions and concerns.*
- *Provide multiple opportunities for parents to communicate in their language and method of preference, such as digital and in-person formats, class visits, phone conversations, text message, email, collaborative projects, and impromptu conferences.*
- *Work with families early and often to gather insight into students' cultures, goals, and learning preferences.*
- *Enact classroom management strategies that avoid assigning blame or guilt to students based on perceptions about their cultures, differences, or home lives.*
- *Work toward creating an environment that establishes mutually agreed-upon norms and encourages students to act out of a sense of personal responsibility to follow those norms, not from a fear of punishment or desire for a reward.*
- *Meet with families to understand and align the recognition, reward, and incentive practices used in the classroom to the values and cultural norms of families.*
- *Create opportunities to allow different groups and ideas to become part of the fabric of the school community by organizing proactive community building circles and activities that promote positive relationships among individuals from diverse backgrounds. Include students, teachers, school staff, leaders, families, and community members in these opportunities.*
- *Use restorative justice circles and structures to welcome students back into learning when harm has occurred.*
- *Participate in the review of school and district policies (codes of conduct, curriculum reviews, community engagement, etc.).*
- *Attend or volunteer at community events, when possible, to develop relationships with families and the community outside of the classroom setting.*
- *Respond to instances of disrespectful speech about student identities by intervening if hurtful speech or slurs are used, addressing the impact of said language, and discussing appropriate and inappropriate responses when instances of bias occur. Use these moments as opportunities to build classroom environments of acceptance.*
- *Identify and address implicit bias in the school and community environment.*
- *Encourage students to take academic risks in order to create an environment that capitalizes on student mistakes as learning opportunities that help students grow academically and emotionally.*

School Leader Version: Creating a Welcoming and Affirming Environment

- *Conduct periodic review of school policies (i.e., dress code, discipline code, conduct code), by collaborating with parents, teachers, community members and incorporating research-based best practices such as restorative justice, positive behavior interventions, and supports.*
- *Assess school climate using a variety of measures (i.e., surveys, interviews, focus groups, informal gatherings) to collect diverse stakeholder impressions and experiences, using questions that consider issues of diversity, equity, and inclusion.*
- *Disaggregate data (i.e., discipline, attendance, enrollment in advanced coursework, special education, and gifted and talented programs) by sub-group, evaluate trends, and create a strategic plan to address disproportionality.*
- *Provide space for teachers and staff to process and determine how to engage with students and families after social and political events that impact the wider community.*
- *Support formal and informal structures for families to receive information about grade-level standards and expectations, developmentally appropriate social emotional tools, and strategies to support academic and social growth at home.*
- *Provide interpretation services at family meetings (i.e., parent organization meetings, community events, during the enrollment process, during the provision of special education services, etc.) to ensure family engagement includes meaningful two-way communication and offers families the opportunity to share (not just receive) in their home language.*
- *Develop multiple means of ongoing family engagement (i.e., apps and online systems of communication, parent leadership opportunities, parent-family liaison positions, opportunities for families to serve as active co-creators of policies and programs, parent organizing bodies, and holding meetings at varied hours, possibly providing transportation and childcare, outreach at community meetings).*
- *Create advisory groups consisting of various education stakeholders (families, teachers, students, community members) to work collaboratively to set school norms, establish school goals, and build alignment between the families' expectations and values, and the school's expectations and values.*
- *Work with cultural and community centers to identify needs and provide services to families by offering classes such as parenting, financial literacy, computer literacy, or English language at the school.*
- *Highlight works of art designed by students and members of the broader community that incorporate relevant cultural and historical context. Create a visibly multilingual and multicultural environment by posting signs, banners, and other materials throughout the school that acknowledge and celebrate the identities of students.*
- *Post high-quality work in the physical environment that is not limited to the display of correct answers, but also demonstrates students' critical thinking, conceptual understanding, reasoning, and application of content to meaningful real-world situations. Work to ensure high-quality work is equitably represented from students across sub-groups.*

- *Create "listening conferences" or "peacemaking circles" led by a trained facilitator through which all stakeholders can discuss cultural and social values and resolve conflict.*
- *Develop peer mediation programs where trained student mediators assist their peers in settling disputes.*
- *Incorporate time in the school day when formal restorative practices can occur.*
- *Provide the time and resources for students to create cultural clubs to learn more about their culture as well as other students' cultures.*
- *Develop interview questions when hiring new staff that provide opportunities for candidates to identify ways they share (or don't share) experiences with the local student populations and to explain the implications of those experiences for their professional practices.*
- *Incorporate parent and community voices into the hiring process.*

REFLECTION QUESTIONS

What do you notice in the two frameworks? What is most pronounced? What is missing?

What does your own commitment to equity with student culture and climate entail?

GUIDING QUESTIONS

Here are some questions to consider as you think about DEI within your student culture and climate work:

- Within your school, network, or district, which profile of student-teacher relationships are the most strained, weak, challenged, or nonexistent? Why is or might this be the case?
- Within your school, network, or district, which profile of student-teacher relationships are the most strong, healthy, and catalytic? Why is or might this be the case?
- To what extent are there different needs among different student profiles within your school, network, or district? How do we accommodate and meet those needs?
- Within your school, network, or district, which profile of student-student relationships are the most strained, weak, challenged, or nonexistent? Why is or might this be the case?
- Within your school, network, or district, which profile of student-student relationships are the most strong, healthy, and catalytic? Why is or might this be the case?
- How does your school, network, or district create spaces (such as restorative circles) to support healthy student-student relationships (which includes helping students resolve conflict)?
- Within your school, network, or district, which profile of administrator-student relationships are the most strained, weak, challenged, or nonexistent? As well as why is or might this be the case?
- Within your school, network, or district, which profiles of administrator-student relationships are the most strong, healthy, and catalytic? As well as why is or might this be the case?
- To what extent do your artifacts center the different identities of the students you serve as a school, network, or district?
- Within your school, network, or district, do your rules, expectations, and policies take into account the different identities of your students?
- Within your school, network, or district, are your rules, expectations, and policies inclusive?
- Within your school, network, or district, are your rules, expectations, and policies equitable?
- Within your school, network, or district, do your consequences take into account the different identities your students hold?
- Within your school, network, or district, do you notice disparities or inequities within your discipline data?
- Within your school, network, or district, are your rewards and incentives mindful of the varying identities and needs of your students?
- Within your school, network, or district, is your student programming mindful of the varying identities and needs of your students?

- How does your physical environment honor the varying identities of your students?
- Within your school, network, or district, who is most represented? Who is least? Who isn't represented within your physical environment at all?
- Within your school, network, or district, whose or what traditions and customs do you preserve and enact?
- Within your school, network, or district, are any traditions and customs culturally insensitive, or insensitive to any particular profile of student?
- Within your school, network, or district, to what extent are the appreciation of differences and principles of inclusion a part of students' core values, mindsets, and beliefs?
- Within your school, network, or district, to what extent do we explicitly teach diversity and inclusion to students so that they model this with one another and with your staff team and other adults?
- Within your school, network, or district, is there any language used that is culturally insensitive or insensitive to any particular profile of student?
- To what extent does your school, network, or district foster a nurturing environment that students want to belong to/be a part of? How do you know?
- As it relates to student behavior and the overall culture encouraged, to what extent does your school, network, or district hold low expectations for students?
- To what extent are your school, network, or district's expectations for students of color different than those for their white counterparts?
- Would the expectations of your school, network, or district for students be considered high expectations in a different school setting (e.g., white, affluent, etc.)?
- To what extent is there evidence of differentiated discipline approaches to address students' needs within your school, network, or district?
- To what extent does your school, network, or district track and monitor your students' social-emotional wellness?
- To what extent are periodic screenings taking place to assess students' needs within your school, network, or district?
- To what extent does your school, network, or district provide targeted intervention for students in need based on assessment data?
- Does your school, network, or district provide multiple strategies to foster safe and supportive school climates for all students and families?
- Do all students in your school, network, or district have the opportunity to partake in social emotional learning opportunities (e.g., social emotional learning curriculum)?
- To what extent does your school, network, or district promote the idea of being "color-blind" in our approach and engagement with students?
- Does your school, network, or district evaluate our student code of conduct and student discipline referral process to ensure it includes safeguards that assess student trauma

manifesting through behaviors (especially for students disproportionately affected by exclusionary discipline policies and economic insecurity)?

- Does your school, network, or district specify support and strategies to meet the needs of English learners?
- Within middle and high school settings, has your school, network, or district offered and normalized student affinity groups across racial lines?
- Does your school, network, or district evaluate how comfortable students feel voicing opinions and expressing behaviors in school?
- To what extent:
  - Do all student identities and voices get recognized equally in your school, network, or district?
  - Do students who are _____ feel emotionally safe?
  - Do students who are _____ feel psychologically safe?
  - Do students who are _____ feel traumatized by any of our practices and/or policies?
  - Do student identities and voices get celebrated in your school, network, or district?
  - Do student identities or voices get discouraged or punished in your school, network, or district?
  - Is student voice allowed to affect policy making in your school, network, or district?
- To what extent does your school, network, or district formally know if _____ students:
  - Are eager to attend our school?
  - Perceive that adults in the school sincerely care about them and their success?
  - Believe they are likely to succeed academically and get what they need at our school?
  - Feel a personal connection to the adults at our school?
- Does your school, network, or district disaggregate discipline data by teacher and infraction?
- Does your school, network, or district identify trends with the data and address those trends with individual teachers?
- Does your school, network, or district have clear, developmentally appropriate, and logical discipline policies and procedures?
- Does your school, network, or district identify alternative discipline programs that support cultural responsiveness and trauma-informed approaches within our discipline?
- Does your school, network, or district eliminate zero tolerance policies that prevent students from maximizing their time in the classroom?
- Does your school, network, or district execute a clear and effective plan in addressing individual teachers/staff that displays discriminatory discipline practices?
- How does your school, network, or district's physical environment reflect, honor, and/or celebrate the identity, history, and heritage of the students we serve?

REFLECTION QUESTIONS

Which of these student culture and climate guiding questions stand out most
to you and why?

If you're currently engaged in DEI work within the arena of student culture
and climate, which of these areas are aspects of strength or visible and/or
meaningful progress for your school, district, nonprofit, or company?

If you're currently engaged in DEI work within the arena of student culture
and climate, which of these areas are aspects of weakness or challenge for your
school, district, nonprofit, or company? Which have you not been as intentional about altogether?

ADDITIONAL RESOURCES

Here are additional tools, frameworks, and resources you can leverage to deepen your understanding of how to foster positive culture and climate generally. In all of the following resources, please be sure to apply an intentional lens of diversity and inclusion to further acknowledge the importance of being hyper-aware as an educational leader of the varying needs of students by identity markers (e.g., LGBTQIA+ youth), as well as students' different unique lived experiences (e.g., students of households with an active duty military parent).

National Center on Safe Supportive Learning Environments (NCSSLE) is funded by the US Department of Education's Office of Safe and Healthy Students. NCSSLE provides resources, training, and technical assistance on school climate and its components to states, grantees, district administrators, schools, teachers and staff members, families, and students. The NCSSLE website highlights the most up-to-date and seminal research on school climate and provides links to related products, tools, and websites.

StopBullying.gov represents a multiagency federal effort to better understand the issue of bullying and how to prevent and respond to it. In addition to the resources provided for parents and other community members, StopBullying.gov features information to help schools educate students and staff members about bullying and implement policies that create an environment of safety.

The US Department of Education's Office of Safe and Healthy Students (OSHS) funds and promotes initiatives, research, and publications on education, health, mental health, safety, and drug and violence prevention. The OSHS website provides an overview of the programs, initiatives, and technical assistance centers administered by The Office of Safe and Healthy Students (OSHS) and highlights relevant events, reports, websites, publications, and other available resources.

Centers for Disease Control and Prevention's Adolescent and School Health: School Connectedness is a webpage that provides a definition of and information on school connectedness and why it is so important.

The Centers for Disease Control and Prevention (CDC) Injury Center works to promote violence and injury prevention by gathering and reporting data, funding programs, and prevention activities, and disseminating resources and tools. The School Violence topic page of the Injury Center provides statistics, risk and protective factors, and information about prevention efforts and tools related to school violence.

SAMPLE NEXT STEPS

Here are examples of actions educational leaders may take as a result of their findings of auditing the state of DEI within student culture and climate across schools:

- As a school, network, or district, create a policy statement about your commitment to culturally responsive sustaining education, and include all staff members (teachers, school safety officers, counselors, lunch and recess workers) in its creation, development, and ongoing training.
- As a school, network, or district, conduct periodic review of school policies (e.g., dress code, discipline code, conduct code) by collaborating with parents, teachers, and community members and incorporating research-based best practices such as restorative justice, positive behavior interventions, and supports.
- As a school, network, or district, encourage and incentivize school leaders to hold spaces (e.g., community forums, social events) that foster collaboration among teachers, families, and community members that provide insight into the assets that exist among the school community.
- As a school, network, or district, provide resources to schools (i.e., shared language, online resources, questions for discussion, etc.) for incorporating and responding to current events and events that affect the community.
- As a school, network, or district, formalize structures for school and district-wide parent collaboration, such as parent-teacher associations/organizations (PTA/PTO) or academic parent-teacher teams (APTT).
- As a school, network, or district, assess school climate using a variety of measures (e.g., surveys, interviews, focus groups, informal gatherings) to collect diverse stakeholder impressions and experiences, using questions that consider issues of DEI.
- As a school, network, or district, disaggregate data (e.g., discipline, attendance, enrollment in advanced coursework, special education, and gifted and talented programs) by sub-group, evaluate trends, and create a strategic plan to address disproportionality.
- As a school, network, or district, make accessible and readable information readily available to families in a variety of modes, including translations and accommodations for those with disabilities.
- As a school, network, or district, provide interpretation services at family meetings (e.g., parent organization meetings, community events, during the enrollment process, during the provision.of special education services, etc.) to ensure family engagement includes meaningful two-way communication and offer families the opportunity to share (not just receive) in their home language.
- As a school, network, or district, gather family and community feedback on district-wide policies before implementation and provide transparent updates during and after implementation.

- As a school, network, or district, develop multiple means of ongoing family engagement (e.g., apps and online systems of communication, holding meetings at varied hours, possibly providing transportation and childcare, outreach at community meetings or other places the community gathers).

- As a school, network, or district, stay current on wider social and political issues that affect communities served by the district (e.g., hold regular meetings with community-based organizations and advocacy groups, create a community liaison role to gather information from the field).

- As a school, network, or district, work to improve the recruitment and retention of a diverse teacher workforce (e.g., teachers who identify as people of color, LGBTQIA+, differently abled) by strengthening pipelines for teacher education and cultivating relationships with local and national partners (e.g., historically Black colleges and universities, Hispanic association of colleges and universities, alliance organizations).

- As a school, network, or district, identify, cultivate, and support students who are interested in joining the district in the future as a classroom teacher or school professional (e.g., school counselor, occupational and speech pathologist, etc.) by partnering with higher education and other professional organizations that could provide scholarships, internships, externships, and mentorship opportunities, as a means to strengthen teacher education pipelines.

- As a school, network, or district, work with cultural and community centers and organizations to identify needs and provide services to families by offering classes such as parenting, financial literacy, computer literacy, or English language at the school.

CHAPTER 9

Operations and Finance

We don't often think of finance, financial management, or even fundraising as playing a role within the work of centering and advancing DEI with the education sector, but rest assured, it is also an essential part of the work. Here are some areas of opportunities to center and advance DEI with finance:

- Funding sources
- Budgeting
- Financial planning
- Financial management
- Procurement
- Compensation
- Resource allocation
- Accounting
- And so much more!

As you work to apply a DEI lens in finance, one of the easiest ways to begin doing so is in championing inclusive procurement practices. Inclusive procurement refers to the process of creating the environment for businesses owned by people of color and/or women and other marginalized communities especially to participate in procurement and/or contracting processes within your school, network, district, nonprofit, or company. Inclusive business participation in any organization's procurement and contracting is an important source of income and jobs in communities of color and other marginalized communities. It really does help to strengthen community partnerships your school, network, district, nonprofit, or company may have, and by default it then honestly also strengthens communities economically and socially.

It also enables you to express your value of DEI with the dollars that you spend. Moreover, educational leaders and systems have a tremendous opportunity to stop assigning little budgets to big commitments when you take on DEI within finance. So often we see DEI work (programming, initiatives, etc.) not be financially supported, yet we want great results and significant progress. Truthfully, that's not equity. It's insanity! I want you to ensure that your budget and financial investment match what you say your DEI priorities are. You can't love _____ (equity, families, wellness, whatever fits the blank for you) and not appropriately fund it.

SAMPLE FRAMEWORK

So, let's dive a bit deeper to one framework that focused on how educational leaders within the finance realm can imagine equity-focused budgeting from Education Resource Strategies (ERS). In 2018, ERS published "Transforming School Funding for Equity, Transparency, and Flexibility: A Nuts-and-Bolts Guide to Implementing Student-Based Budgeting" guide. Following is an excerpt:

> *Student-based budgeting (SBB) goes by many names, including student-based allocations (SBA), fair student funding (FSF), weighted student funding (WSF), or student-centered funding (SCF). Regardless of the name, at its core SBB is a funding system whereby dollars follow students based on student need. More specifically, it describes any district funding model that:*
>
> - *Allocates dollars instead of staff or materials*
> - *Is based on the number of students*
> - *Uses objective and measurable student characteristics as weights SBB differs from the traditional funding system used in most American school districts, where resources are distributed to schools in the form of staff and dollars designated for specific purposes. As a result, principals in traditional systems have limited flexibility over their resources. Many districts provide little transparency as to why schools get what they get, which makes it difficult to assess how equitably the funding system allocates resources.*
>
> *In contrast, SBB is designed to promote the three pillars of a high-performing funding system:*
>
> - *Equity: "Dollars follow the student." The strongest funding models ensure that resources are distributed equitably based on student need.*
> - *Transparency: "The formula tells you what you get." The optimal funding system has clear and easily understood rules for where, how, and why dollars flow. Under SBB, these rules are expressed as a formula.*
> - *Flexibility: "Principals own their budgets." By distributing funds rather than staff, SBB enables school leaders to define the resources they need to drive student achievement.*
>
> *A real school might receive more or less money under SBB than under a traditional model, depending on a number of factors; a real school would likely receive*

additional funding sources beyond just the SBB allocation; and a principal certainly would not make complex budget trade-offs and school design decisions without support. Nonetheless, it captures the core distinctions between the two approaches. In a traditional budget, each school receives a set allocation, which may not account for the unique needs of each school's population, and may not adequately fund schools that serve a high-need population. In an SBB system, the district determines an SBB formula that typically includes a base weight (a dollar-per-pupil amount that all students receive), as well as student need weights (additional funding to students with additional needs). The characteristics and dollar amounts that systems choose for their student need weights are a reflection of their concept of equity. Schools then receive an SBB dollar allocation based on the school's enrollment and the district's SBB formula, and then the principal determines which resources the school needs.

As discussed in "Transforming School Funding for Equity, Transparency, and Flexibility: An Introduction to Student-Based Budgeting," SBB is more than a funding system—it is a way to empower schools to make big changes on behalf of their students. This requires concrete shifts in the jobs of both school and district office staff, as well as broader shifts in how staff conceptualize their roles and the roles of their colleagues. These shifts in actions and mindsets are key for making real change in school practices, and they do not happen organically. For SBB to be successful, you must explicitly manage this change in roles for staff across the district. In a traditional system, principals often serve as building and HR managers, enacting a vision largely set by the district and working within the resources provided to them. In an SBB system, principals will now make decisions about how a majority of resources are used and organized, based on their overall budget and the needs and priorities of their school. This means principals will spend more time on the school budgeting process and will need to build the skills to make hard resource trade-offs and find creative solutions. This requires a new investment in principal training and onboarding (discussed further in phase 3, "Prepare for and Complete the Rollout"). With this increased autonomy, principals may also experience greater accountability for student outcomes. At the same time, the district office must adapt from a traditional "command and control center," where staff are mandating decisions to principals about what resources they will receive and how they will be used, to a "collaborative service center." In an SBB system, the district office will play more of a customer service role, seeking to support principals in realizing their vision with the budgets they have, even in times when the principal vision is different from their own. This will require cross-department coordination, a collaborative problem-solving mindset, and a level of trust in the decisions that principals are making. District office staff will directly control fewer school resource decisions. Instead, they will spend more time helping principals solve issues that are most pressing to them. They will influence school practices through the support they provide, as well as by documenting and sharing best practices across the district. At the same time, district staff will remain responsible for ensuring compliance with any local, state, or federal regulations across schools, determining the non-negotiables for all schools in the district, and holding schools accountable for results. The process to redefine roles and shift mindsets will certainly take time, and there is no one right path. Potential actions to support this shift include:

- *Recognize this shift and identify potential pain points in your district. For example, if you recognize that there currently isn't much cross-departmental collaboration, you can begin to foster that change early in the process.*
- *Describe and document the principal and district office role you desire and share that vision widely. If you're asking people to do their jobs differently, they need to understand what you're actually asking them to do.*
- *Engage teams around this shift and their new roles to build clarity on and comfort with these new expectations.*
- *Design your formula with the desired roles in mind—that is, if you envision the principal's role to be that of the core decision maker at schools, then they need flexibility over sufficient resources to be able to make meaningful decisions.*
- *Consider changes to district office roles and structures. To best serve schools in this new role, district offices may need to organize themselves differently. Some districts choose to create new roles, such as "budget partner" or "HR partner," to provide direct support to principals. These roles are focused on facilitating the budgeting and staffing process for school leaders, which requires a broad knowledge of compliance rules across different departments. Districts may also create cross-functional network support teams with individuals from different departments who all support the same group of schools. This fosters cross-departmental collaboration and creates a unified source of support for principals.*

REFLECTION QUESTIONS

What do you notice in this framework ? As an educational leader, what captures your attention, and why?

> **What does this make you think about your own budgeting processes?**
>
>

GUIDING QUESTIONS

So, now let's look at what central or guiding questions you can consider as an educational leader within this area of your school, network, or district's work:

- Does your school, network, or district prioritize contracting with vendors and partners led by people of color or with a mission related to racial equity?
- Does your school, network, or district prioritize contracting with woman-owned vendors or any partners with a mission that drives gender equity?
- Does your school, network, or district prioritize contracting with local vendors or any partners who reside within your city, state, or local region?
- In terms of vending, will your organization have any type of minority, women and emerging small business policy to support vendors from marginalized groups?
- Do you routinely capture data (disaggregated by race) on who your organization contracts with?
- If your organization has equity practices and policies, will you require your vendors and contractors to adhere to the same practices and policies?
- How can your racial justice values influence your organization's financial investments and/or overall spending?
- In what ways can you ensure that your organization's budget allocations are aligned with racial equity goals, plans, policies, and/or values?
- If you're a nonprofit, what explicit DEI goals can you incorporate into your fundraising strategy and practices?
- Will your organization provide transparent salary bands?
- To what extent is there an equitable pay scale/compensation structure in place?
- Do you have plans to fund racial equity initiatives so that resources—including consultants, training programs, and one-on-one coaching—are available to grow your staff members' or team's capacity?

- What percentage of your current spend goes to local vendors?
- What percentage of your current spend goes to vendors of color?
- Is there any way that you collect feedback on the experiences vendors of marginalized groups have with your organization?
- How do you set vendors up for success in obtaining contracts with your organization? Is there equitable access to information? Is there a formal and fair process for procurement?
- Is all contract language or RFP language explicit about your organization's commitment to racial equity?
- Will your organizational materials be assessed for racial bias and other forms of bias? If so, who will do it?
- Do you have a method in place to assess the overall satisfaction of communities of color with your organization (e.g., those you serve or even those you do not)?
- Consider your organization's primary physical space and what it may communicate to diverse stakeholders. Is it welcoming and accessible?
- How can you ensure that your primary physical space is welcoming and supportive of diverse individuals and families; for example, is there comfortable seating and supports for those with children?
- What is the intended purpose of _____ (a particular service, product, or program)? Why was it created (i.e., history)?
- Who informed its need, content, structure, components, goals, and so on?
- To what extent are outcomes able to be predetermined along racial lines?
- What are its current metrics? How often are they monitored?
- How do we analyze _____'s data and allow that information to inform our decision-making? Do we feel that we are measuring what matters?
- What market research have we conducted within marginalized identity groups for the services, products, and/or programming we are seeking to provide (be it formal or informal)? Or are we making assumptions in any way about what a particular demographic wants or actually needs?
- In what ways do your products, services, and/or programming meet discrete needs of communities of color or other marginalized groups?
- Is there demand for the product, service, and/or programming? How do you know?
- Where are your customers physically located? Is there a means of transport and delivery for the product idea for that target group, or will you have to be imaginative and build new distribution partnerships?

REFLECTION QUESTIONS

As you consider your school or organization's financial work, which guiding questions capture your attention the most and why?

Which guiding question represents a growth area for you and/or your school, district, nonprofit, company, or organization?

Which guiding question represents an area of strength for you and/or your school, district, nonprofit, company, or organization?

SAMPLE NEXT STEPS

Sample action items that may come from taking the time to audit and analyze the extent to which DEI is centered within your school or district's finance and operations include the following:

- Create DEI goals for your vending or procurement work as a venture.
- Prioritize contracting with vendors and partners led by people of color, as well as local vendors of color in particular.
- Conduct a financial equity audit to assess your organization's current baseline of procurement practices across various identity markers.
- Allot a specific line item of your budget to racial equity or DEI initiatives.
- Do not practice asking vendors of color for discounted rates/pricing when you do not ask the same of white vendors.
- Assess all programs, goods, and services for racial bias or other forms of bias.
- Assess the overall satisfaction of communities of color and other marginalized groups within your organization's services, products, or programming.
- Instead of assuming what any group needs, ask them. Conduct market research within marginalized identity groups for the services, products, and/or programming they are seeking or need.

Family and Community Engagement

When you think of family and community engagement, it's important to first examine the beliefs you hold about the role of parents, guardians, and community stakeholders within the process of educating our children. The art and science of centering and advancing DEI in this area begins with asset-based thinking in the inherent value of parents, families, and community to the educational process. We must believe that regardless of skin color, educational attainment level, and other identity markers, they have rich insight, perspective, and lived experiences that can enhance the quality of our schools, systems, nonprofits, and companies.

We must consider the representation of the various families and community stakeholders we serve and what their hopes and dreams are for their students as well as our schools. We must consider what their needs and concerns are. We must consider which of our families are at an inherent disadvantage and which are at an advantage with how our school, system, nonprofit, or company functions. We must consider the extent to which we privy certain voices and whose voice we do not. We must consider the various profiles of families and community stakeholders we serve.

SAMPLE FRAMEWORKS

Here is an excerpt from a framework created by the American Institutes for Research under the US Department of Education. Published in December 2018, it is entitled "Strategies for Equitable Family Engagement" and is a really wonderful guide that helps educators reimagine family engagement to drive equity.

> ### Making a Commitment to Equitable Family Engagement
> *By making a clear and transparent commitment to equitable family engagement in both public communications and leadership activities, school and district leaders can encourage school staff and families to build and strengthen communication and engagement systems. School and district leaders may consider the following strategies for making a commitment to equitable family engagement.*

Plan strategically over time.

Practicing equitable family engagement requires an intentional, long-term effort to change ingrained perceptions, beliefs, and regular practices of school staff. This is not an effort schools can undertake on their own; to be successful, school staff will need to work with families and the community to facilitate communication, trust, and changes in practice over time. These efforts are most effective when student progress and family engagement is perceived by both families and school staff as a "shared responsibility," underscored by mutual respect (SEDL & U.S. Department of Education, 2013). Establishing a shared responsibility for family engagement requires school leaders to commit to learning from and with families about how to effectively engage with each other over time, rather than approaching engagement as a "top-down" initiative. This may require school leaders to codify equitable family engagement as a major component of their school success criteria, for example:

- *Clearly articulating a vision for equitable family engagement*
- *Establishing family engagement standards and holding staff accountable for meeting these standards*
- *Supporting staff in developing new mindsets, skills, and practices related to equitable family engagement*
- *Examining and modifying policies, as appropriate, that affect family engagement*
- *Reallocating resources, as appropriate, for family engagement*
- *Monitoring progress and evaluating success in promoting equitable family engagement over time (Nuri-Robbins et al., 2007)*

Offer professional learning on cultural responsiveness for school staff.

For equitable family engagement to be the norm, school staff need to be aware of key concepts such as implicit bias and identity; likewise, school staff need to effectively use cognitive and emotional processes related to cultural responsiveness such as social-emotional skills (Richards, Brown, & Ford, 2007). Through professional learning, school staff can develop key knowledge and skills related to equitable family engagement, including how to effectively:

- *Model and advocate for valuing diversity.*
- *Self-assess and demonstrate awareness of one's own identity and culture within the broader school and community context.*
- *Promote culturally competent teaching and family engagement practices, including distinguishing between behavioral challenges and cultural differences.*
- *Promote and teach students communication and conflict resolution skills related to cultural differences.*
- *Understand and utilize appropriate and effective family engagement strategies. (Nuri-Robbins et al., 2007)*

Pursue human resource strategies that will attract diverse educators and family engagement staff.

It is important to have school and district staff that understand (and where possible, reflect) the school community to help inclusive family engagement become standard practice. Having diverse school staff that reflect the background or cultures of the broader school community can often accelerate improvements in communication, relationships, and interactions with families by allowing staff to learn from each other (Camino, 1992). It is important to note that while having a racially or culturally diverse staff of educators can sometimes facilitate better cross-cultural dialogue or build social trust with families, hiring a diverse staff of educators is not a sufficient strategy by itself for facilitating inclusive family engagement (Boser, 2014). Schools and districts can also hire staff at the school and district levels who are specifically responsible for guiding and managing family engagement. These dedicated staff can provide helpful support to educators and promote the use of more effective, consistent, and equitable strategies across classrooms and schools.

Ensure communications are accessible to all families.

Limited English proficiency is one of the greatest barriers to school engagement, and providing interpreters is part of a school's civil rights requirements. Likewise, written communications (including websites, newsletters, and direct family communications) must be provided in all relevant home languages to ensure families are directly informed. Using students as interpreters and translators may violate civil rights requirements and may create a negative power dynamic among students, parents, and school staff (e.g., when students are responsible for translating information about their own behavior or performance). While students may be able to navigate cultural differences between teachers and families, having students serve as the primary communicator with families can be perceived as a challenge to authority by family members, potentially exacerbating communication challenges (McDevitt & Butler, 2011).

Offer structures to listen to families.

In addition to self-reflection and professional development, teachers, school leaders, and district staff may benefit from intentional structures that allow them to practice listening to families over time. In many schools, communication may be primarily initiated by the teacher; however, schools that establish regular listening sessions with families can help teachers improve their listening and relational skills with families and the community. Some of the most successful parent engagement strategies have involved community liaisons or trusted advocate programs that capitalize on the value of community members that speak the language and are of the same culture.

Engage with community organizations.

Families may engage in learning activities that occur outside of school, such as community-based enrichment or tutoring programs. Some of these programs are evidence-based and beneficial to students, but school staff are often not aware of student participation in these activities unless notified by family members (Stephens & Pate, 2015). Schools may benefit from networking with local churches, community organizations, and neighborhood libraries, leveraging existing programs and events to share information with families and show support for learning activities that happen outside of school. Some family members may also feel more comfortable engaging in a peer group and in a neutral, trusted space (Finigan-Carr, Copeland-Linder, Haynie, & Cheng, 2014).

Communicate based on cultural norms and priorities.

Families communicate and engage in a variety of different ways; for some schools, there may be significant differences between typical communication practices and family preferences (e.g., families preferring texting rather than after-school calls or informal conversations rather than formal conferences). Using only a limited range of communication methods can hinder family engagement over time. Adapting communications to reflect both school and family cultural norms and priorities can make it easier for families to engage and help school staff build rapport and trust with families. In practice, the local norms to include or consider in communications may vary depending on the specific culture or community.

Building on the previous framework, the next framework is an excerpt from Learning for Justice (formerly Teaching Tolerance)'s "Best Practices for Serving English Language Learners" guide, which was published in 2017.

Do

Be clear about the purpose of meetings. Set goals and communicate them prior to every meeting or conversation so teachers and families have shared, realistic expectations.

Be mindful of the potential power differential between parents or guardians and teachers. Negative past experiences (as either a student or a parent), immigration status, different cultural norms and expectations, and lack of English language fluency can cause discomfort and lead families to disengage from the school.

Provide a translator if you don't speak the parents' or guardians' primary language fluently. The nuance and detail necessary to convey how adult family members might best engage in the student's education should be communicated in the family's primary language.

Start the meeting on a positive note. Try to find an area where the student is doing well academically, socially, athletically, etc. Beginning the meeting with what is wrong or what needs improvement diminishes trust and can make parents feel defensive and anxious about their child's prospects at the school.

Use terms that everyone understands. If there are some concepts or terms that need explanation, provide necessary detail and consider providing additional preparatory materials to families in advance of the scheduled meeting. Avoid acronyms and jargon.

Visit the family in their home. The goal of this practice is to learn about how knowledge is transmitted in the student's home, to get to know the family, and to discover their expectations related to schools and teachers, and to understand the family's academic goals for their child.

Don't

Use the student as the translator. Even if parent-teacher conferences are student led, they may well become misled if parents and teachers are unable to communicate independently. Using the student as the translator can put the student in an awkward position where loyalty and respect for their teachers and their family can feel contradictory.

Assume that any bilingual adult will be a successful translator.

Using families of other students, or other students themselves, compromises privacy. What is gained in increased clarity will be lost if families feel embarrassed or disrespected.

Language Access

Offering translation or interpretation services to families who do not speak or understand English fluently sends a welcoming message and supports successful home-school relationships. In public school settings, offering these services is also a legal obligation: Districts must ensure that all staff communicate with families in a language they can understand and notify families of any program, service, or activity communicated to English-speaking families. For "major" languages (top languages spoken) in a district, a full array of language access should be provided. For "lower incidence" languages (languages spoken less frequently), a district can offer interpretation only.

Planning 101: District-wide Language Access Services

Administrators and staff can use best practices to create a comprehensive communication plan for families of ELL students.

- *Identify the district's "major" versus "lower incidence" languages.*
- *Utilize appropriate staff; if necessary, reach out to the community to fill service gaps.*
- *Post signs in high-traffic areas of every school about interpretation services.*

- *Distribute written information on how to request translation or interpretation services to every parent or guardian during enrollment and registration.*
- *Have the bank of teacher report card comments translated.*
- *Prepare to address common scenarios or to host big events in multiple languages.*
- *Consider organizing a district-level bilingual parent advisory committee.*

What Gets Translated and Interpreted?

Written & Translated

- *Handbooks, policies, and forms*
- *Discipline policies*
- *Disciplinary notices*
- *Report cards and other academic performance notes*
- *Parent/guardian permission forms*
- *Grievance procedures*
- *Bullying notices*
- *Notices about school choice*
- *Nondiscrimination notices*
- *Testing accommodations*
- *Registration documents and home language survey*
- *"Change of Address or Telephone" form*
- *"Student Not Riding Bus" form*
- *"Reason for Absence" form*
- *"Request for Conference" form*
- *"Early Dismissal" form*

Verbal & Interpreted

- *Registration and enrollment process*
- *Counseling on eligibility for ELL program*
- *Disciplinary hearings*
- *Orientation and back-to-school events*
- *Family-teacher conferences*
- *Medical emergencies and nurse calls*
- *Schoolwide announcements over the intercom*
- *Special education meetings*
- *Helping family report absences*
- *Testing accommodations*

PRINCIPLES TO GUIDE YOUR COMMUNITY ENGAGEMENT EFFORTS

A partnership is any formal or informal relationship you build with external individuals or institutions that advances your school or organizational mission, vision, and goals. Strong partnerships are relationships that are built on clarity, mutual benefit, and mutual trust. Here are some overarching themes you'll want to consider on the journey to become a more diverse, equitable, and inclusive school community.

Continuous Learning

As it relates to equity, it is important to see yourselves as constant learners on the journey of becoming equitable and inclusive practitioners, leaders, advocates, and more. Embrace learning alongside and from other organizations.

Organizational Self-Awareness

In order to partner with organizations to advance inclusive entrepreneurship, it is essential that organizations consider, for instance, (1) their local, regional, and/or national reputation and past history as it relates to modeling and promoting DEI; (2) your school or organization's internal capacity (i.e., time, resources, talent, etc.); and (3) power dynamics (i.e., what influence, privilege, advantages, etc. that one might carry as an organization in relationship to others).

Clarity

It is vital to prioritize time and energy seeking clarity on a number of essential attributes and characteristics of the partnership one seeks to build and maintain. These include, but are not limited to (1) what one defines as partnership and (2) the degree of capacity available.

Mutual Accountability and Satisfaction

It is important that both organizations hold one another accountable to the outcomes that have been agreed on, particularly in the allocation of time, money, efforts, and other resources.

CONSIDERATIONS

- What resources, time, and energy will it require of you? Your partners must make the same considerations.
- Who is determining current capacity?
- How are resources, energy, and time allocated in the organization?
- How do we avoid tokenism?

- Do we have the skill sets or readiness to take on the work (acknowledgment of time, mental and emotional labor, etc.)?
- Are we good at it?
- Does it align with your school or organization's mission, vision, strategic plan, strategies, theory of change, logic model, and so on?
- Does the community need or want it?
- Is it the right time?
- Do we have the capacity (time, funding, resources, and staff) to execute?
- Is there funder interest? Sustained interest? Can we get funders interested in this initiative?
- Will doing it or not doing it cause some/significant organizational risk or risk to our school?
- Are there others already doing it that we can learn from?
- Can someone else do it better, or should we encourage someone else to do it?
- Are all racial/ethnic groups who are affected by the policy/practice/decision at the table?
- How will this partnership affect our students?
- How will this partnership affect our families?
- How will this partnership be perceived by our stakeholders?
- Might this partnership worsen or ignore existing disparities?
- Based on these responses, what revisions are needed in this partnership under discussion?
- What is your partner committing to do?
- What are you committing to do and when?
- How do you handle accountability (i.e., if one of us doesn't meet a commitment or expectation)?
- How do you or will you handle public acknowledgment?
- How do you want to talk about each other?
- How do you express appreciation for one another?
- What would make you feel like this partnership is a success?
- Is this partnership worth your time, effort, energy, and so on?
- Are you able to be mutually accountable to each other?
- Are you both satisfied?

REFLECTION QUESTIONS

What do you notice in the framework above? As an educational leader, what captures your attention, and why?

> **What does this make you think about your own family and community engagement efforts?**
>
>

GUIDING QUESTIONS

- Has our organization explicitly defined who our community is (e.g., who are our community stakeholders—both individuals, groups, and organizations)?
- What are the profiles of families we serve?
- To what extent are our organization's vision and values/were your organization's vision and values developed in conjunction with local community or family stakeholders?
- To what extent does our organization foster a nurturing environment that community members want to belong to/be a part of? How do we know?
- To what extent does our organization foster a nurturing environment that family members want to belong to/be a part of? How do we know?
- Does your organization have formal partnerships with organizations of color or other marginalized groups?
- Does your organization allocate resources for engagement and outreach to varying types or demographics of families or communities?
- In what ways are families formally recognized as key stakeholders in select aspects of our decision-making?
- Are there any community stakeholders that you involve in any of your school decision-making?
- How do you ensure that your community engagement practices with communities of color are culturally appropriate for particular communities of color?
- Does our organization specify established channels of communication with community partners?
- Does your school diversify its communication methods with families?
- How does your organization formally collaborate with community-based organizations to determine and address your organization's responsiveness to the needs of your community stakeholders?
- Do you provide language interpreter/translator services for people who speak languages other than English?

- To what extent does our organization conduct formal or informal needs assessments annually (or per a different level of frequency) to determine the needs of our community? Or, do we automatically assume that we know what their needs are?
- To what extent does our organization engage community voices within particular decision-making processes? If so, how?
- To what extent does our organization engage family voices within particular decision-making processes? If so, how?
- Does our organization assess the effectiveness of our communication with our community?
- Does our organization assess the effectiveness of your family engagement efforts with your families?
- Does our organization understand and assess the perception of our organization within our community?
- Are there designated staff members who create a coordinated plan and execute oversight of community engagement?
- Are there designated staff members who create a coordinated plan and execute oversight of family engagement?
- Does our organization establish opportunities for committees that involve community-based input?
- Does our organization establish opportunities for committees that involve family-based input?

SAMPLE ACTION ITEMS

Here are examples of action items that incorporate increasing intentionality in the areas of family and community engagement:

- Create a clear community engagement plan that authentically incorporates community voice, input, and perspectives.
- Define what community you/your organization are serving. Be specific.
- Post or share materials within multiple languages if you are seeking to reach diverse linguistic audiences.
- Establish formal and most importantly mutually beneficial relationships with organizations of color within your local community.

CHAPTER 11

Marketing, Branding, and Communications

Our marketing and branding efforts—how we brand our school or organization and how we communicate both internally and externally—matter. These efforts can intentionally attract a more diverse audience to our school community or detract them. This includes recruiting and being able to enroll a more diverse student body, being able to recruit and hire a more diverse staff, and being able to attract even diverse funding sources and other types of resources to help further and progress student outcomes.

The way we communicate both internally and externally can also have the same effects. When communication is poor internally, that translates to confusion, resentment, mistrust, and overall dysfunction within a school community among staff from grade team members to school leadership team members and more. For some, the extremely worst conditions of this, particularly when it involves staff members from marginalized communities, such as people of color, members of the LGBTQIA+ community, those whose gender identification may be different from the dominant gender representation of your school or organization, neurodivergent people, and other identity groups, can cause them to feel othered, ostracized, left out, not respected, or not truly feel a sense of belonging. Although this totally intersects with Chapter 6, which focuses on HR, we must be intentional about ensuring that our school, nonprofit, company, or organization's communications leaders understand and infuse a purposeful lens of DEI in everything they do, as well as our HR leaders.

From a marketing and branding standpoint, it is not uncommon to see posts on social media channels or websites of a school's commitment to DEI. However, a beautifully graphic design that communicates Black Lives Matter means nothing for a school, nonprofit, or company if the actual people who identify as Black and work there are not treated on a daily basis as if their voices truly matter. No amount of website posts about a school or organization's commitment to the psychological, emotional, and physical safety of transgendered youth will matter if their actual presence and existence within classroom spaces is met with immense microaggressions by adults within their own school building.

If you're in a position of leadership or decision-making within any type of organizational marketing, branding, or communications, never forget that your words alone hold no power without action that demonstrates what you've said. Within the capacity you have, I ask that you play your part in providing peer accountability to colleagues, managers, supervisors, as well as those in more executive or senior-level positions within your school, system, nonprofit, or company to ensure that your marketing, branding, and overall communication efforts align to what is practiced. In other words, a long and robust action plan holds no power if you all haven't done one ounce of it or infrequently or inconsistently use or leverage it. So, if you are a member of any DEI committee, working group, or a singular position devoted to DEI even related to external relations within your communications responsibilities, make sure to help support the auditing of your institution, actual change of practices and policies where they are needed, and the capacity building (learning and development) of your school, district, nonprofit, or company as a whole.

GUIDING QUESTIONS

- How does your organization market, brand and/or message your equity initiatives?
- Will your organization post visible signs of your organization's commitment to equity in your primary physical location, for example, signage that states your commitment and/or physical representation of diverse communities, on your website, and so on?
- Who (what social identities) are most represented within your external marketing efforts, artifacts, and so on?
- What does your marketing (across different platforms and in different avenues) communicate to communities of color and other marginalized groups (both consciously and unconsciously)?
- Who are you specifically looking to reach? Why them?
- What will the introduction of your brand be to diverse targets and why?
- How prepared are people already for what you're proposing? Do you need to educate the market in any way (accessibility/awareness building)?
- Do you have distinctive values? How do they make your brand and work stand out to marginalized groups?
- What will consumers see in you that they value?
- Who will you not do business with?
- Why will what you stand for motivate consumers of color and other audiences of various social identities to buy or engage with your venture?
- What do you want to come to be known for? (In other words, what's your reputational goal?
- Where will they find you? And why will they want to find you there?
- How will they recognize you? (Is it clear what sector you're part of—but also obvious that you're not the same as everyone else?
- What does your name say about your business model? And what does it say about your culture?

REFLECTION QUESTIONS

As you consider your school or organization's marketing and branding work, which guiding questions capture your attention the most and why?

As you consider your school or organization's internal and external communications, which guiding questions capture your attention the most and why?

Which guiding question represents a growth area for you and/or your school, district, nonprofit, company, or organization?

> **Which guiding question represents an area of strength for you and/or your school, district, nonprofit, company, or organization?**

SAMPLE ACTION ITEMS

- Hire a marketing subject matter expert to conduct an equity audit of your marketing department, efforts, or existing marketing plan(s).
- Post visible signs of your organization's commitment to equity in your primary physical location (e.g., signage that states your commitment and/or physical representation of diverse communities, on your website, etc.).
- Conduct an environmental or community scan of your venture's perception and reputation to better understand how you are perceived (and/or received) by varying groups across lines of racial, socioeconomic, linguistic, and other differences.

PART

Three

Looking Ahead

In Part 3, we focus on taking action in a meaningful way to ensure that your journey is both effective and accountable. From action planning tips to suggestions of professional learning materials to a DEI glossary in the backmatter, this part of the book equips you to move and shift "from awareness building and analysis to action and accountability," in the words of Dr. Barbara J. Love.

Where to Go from Here

No amount of money, efforts, training, or initiatives will change a leader or organization that refuses to do the work. Until you're ready to admit that you have a problem, have contributed to the problem, and are willing to accept what changing looks like, your work will *always* be a bandage to your organization's challenges. Once a leader or organization is ready to engage in the work, I believe that you'll be able to use the content in this work to help drive toward meaningful organizational change.

Here is what I recommend:

- Determine who will be engaged in this work. Are you doing this work alone (which we highly recommend you not, but we do understand that depending on your context or situation it may have to start that way)? Are you forming a working group?
- Build your and your team's awareness of DEI—particularly across different domains. It's really important that you create shared language and conceptual understanding as a team.
- Be willing and ready to engage in your own inner work. There is no way that you'll be able to take this on at the departmental, school, organizational, or institutional levels if you are not engaged in looking at the person in the mirror (you), your own mindsets/ beliefs, actions, and being willing to own your own error, problematic behaviors, or contributions to the furtherance of inequity, injustice, and harm of any type.
- Prioritize which aspects of DEI—as well as what type—will be your focus.
- Decide how you'd like to audit each of the core buckets or domains of focus you have chosen. You may decide to have your core leadership team members use some of the guiding questions featured in this book in order to maximize the input of multiple voices, lenses, and perspectives. You may choose to answer questions via a whole staff survey. It all depends on the type of information you are seeking to gather. You'll want to get an accurate understanding of where your school, district, nonprofit, and company falls on addressing the topic or matter centered within each guiding question.

Note that each guiding question in this book can be converted to an actual action item itself. Using this book as a resource, note which questions are your strengths, which areas are in progress or solid (e.g., this means that there is adequate action taking place in this area, but this does not mean that it is strong, excellent, or exemplary in quality, implementation, or results), and what your areas for improvement are.

In the process of your auditing, you'll need to continue creating channels for receipt of feedback from those with whom you work and serve. Organizations that feel threatened by questions often send a loud message that they don't truly care for feedback. Leaders don't ask for survey completion, open comments, questions, or other forms of data collection, if you're not going to *do* anything with it. Questions from your staff members, parents, students, residents, constituents, or whomever you serve are not a threat. They are actually a form of support *and* accountability. If being asked questions threatens your ego, check yourself. You're there to meet the needs of those you're serving, so it's not possible to meet a need that you *refuse* to either listen to or believe and act on.

- Of the growth areas you note, select two or three areas to establish as priorities for your organization for the quarter or year ahead (e.g., determine the time frame that feels most appropriate and relevant).
- Create an action plan that denotes the following for each of your priorities:
  - What you'd like to achieve or accomplish in that area
  - Strategies
  - What actions or steps you'll take to get there
  - Owners
  - Who will own or do what
  - Timeline
  - When actions or steps will take place
- Once you've created an action plan for your team, establish a time and space to regularly visit your plan to monitor progress, adjust course, as well as celebrate your wins and successes along the way. Even small wins and traction matters. Follow-up and follow-through are critical.

CHAPTER 13

Tools You Can Leverage

Although this chapter is in no way exhaustive, it contains a listing of a few additional resources and tools you can leverage as you, your school, district, nonprofit, or organization take deeper steps into your DEI journey. This list is specifically geared to help you learn more about specific lived experiences. I've organized them by topic; they are all forms or types of diversity.

ABILITY AND EXCEPTIONALITY

- *Demystifying Disability: What to Know, What to Say, and How to Be an Ally* by Emily Ladau (2021)
- *Being Heumann* by Judith Heumann (2020)
- *Exile and Pride* by Eli Claire (2015)
- *Native American Communities on Health and Disability* by Lavonna L. Lovern and Carol Locust (2013)
- *Being Mortal* by Atul Gawande (2014)
- *This Chair Rocks* by Ashton Applewhite (2016)
- *Disability Visibility: First-Person Stories from the Twenty-First Century* by Alice Wong (2020)
- *The Next America* by Paul Taylor and Pew Research Center Staff (2014)
- *Women Rowing North* by Mary Pipher (2019)
- *You Don't Look Your Age . . .* by Sheila Nevins (2017)

DIGITAL LITERACY

- *Artificial Unintelligence: How Computers Misunderstand the World* by Meredith Broussard (2018)
- *Automating Inequality: How High-tech Tools Profile, Police, and Punish the Poor* by Virginia Eubanks (2018)
- *Coded Bias*, directed by Shalini Kantayya (Netflix documentary, 2020)

- *Hello World: Being Human in the Age of Algorithms* by Hannah Fry (2018)
- "How I'm Fighting Bias in Algorithms" by Joy Buolamwini (TEDx Talk, 2016)
- *Masked by Trust: Bias in Library Discovery* by Matthew Reidsma (2019)
- *Information Literacy for Today's Diverse Students* by Alex Berrio Matamoros (2018)

RACE AND ETHNICITY

- *An African American and Latinx History of the United States* by Paul Ortiz (2018)
- *Algorithms of Oppression* by Safiya Umoja Noble (2018)
- *The Dreamkeepers: Successful Teachers of African American Children* by Gloria Ladson-Billings (2009)
- *Between the World and Me* by Ta-Nehisi Coates (2015)
- *Caste: The Origins of Our Discontents* by Isabel Wilkerson (2020)
- *Enrique's Journey* by Sonia Nazario (2013)
- *The Half Has Never Been Told* by Edward E. Baptist (2014)
- *Just Mercy* by Bryan Stevenson (2014)
- *Mediocre: The Dangerous Legacy of White Male America* by Ijeoma Oluo (2020)
- *The New Jim Crow* by Michelle Alexander (2012)
- *Stamped from the Beginning* by Ibram X. Kendi (2016)
- *This Is the Fire: What I Say to My Friends About Racism* by Don Lemon (2021)
- *Waking up White, and Finding Myself in the Story of Race* by Debby Irving (2014)
- *White Rage: The Unspoken Truth of Our Racial Divide* by Carol Anderson (2017)
- *Why Are All the Black Kids Sitting Together in the Cafeteria?* by Beverly Daniel Tatum (2003)

FAITH AND RELIGION

- *Letters to a Young Muslim* by Omar Saif Ghobash (2017)
- *Religious Identity and Renewal in the Twenty-First Century* edited by Simone Sinn and Michael Reid Trice (2016)
- *Welcome to the Episcopal Church* by Christopher Webber (1999)
- *The Indestructible Jews* by Max Dimont (2014)
- *Gautama Buddha: In Life and Legend* by Betty Kelen (2014)

SEXUAL ORIENTATION

- *An Archive of Hope* by Harvey Milk (2013)
- *Not Straight, Not White* by Kevin J. Mumford (2016)
- *The Queer and Transgender Resilience Workbook* by Anneliese Singh (2018)

- *Religious Freedom, LGBT Rights, and the Prospects for Common Ground* edited by William N. Eskridge Jr. and Robin Fretwell Wilson (2019)
- *The Stonewall Reader* edited by New York Public Library (2019)
- *Violence Against Queer People* by Doug Meyer (2015)
- *Sex, Gender, Gender Identity and Gender Discrimination Bad Feminist* by Roxanne Gay (2014)

GENDER

- *Eloquent Rage: A Black Feminist Discovers Her Superpower* by Brittney Cooper (2018)
- *Transgender 101: A Simple Guide to a Complex Issue* by Nicholas M. Tech (2012)
- *It Feels Good to Be Yourself: A Book About Gender Identity* by Theresa Thorn (2019)
- *Excluded* by Julia Serano (2013)
- *Gender Queer: A Memoir* by Maia Kobabe (2019)
- *Feminism Is for Everybody* by bell hooks (2000)
- *None of the Above* by I. W. Gregorio (2015)
- *Gender Born, Gender Made: Raising Healthy Gender-Nonconforming Children* by Diane Ehrensaft (2011)
- *The Riddle of Gender* by Deborah Rudacille (2005)
- *The Right to Be Out: Sexual Orientation and Gender Identity in America's Public Schools* by Stuart Biegel (2010)
- *We Should All Be Feminists* by Chimamanda Ngozi Adichie (2015)

SOCIOECONOMIC STATUS

- *$2.00 a Day* by Kathryn J. Edin and H. Luke Shaefer (2015)
- *The Death Gap: How Inequality Kills* by David A. Ansell (2017)
- *Evicted* by Matthew Desmond (2016)
- *Heartland* by Sarah Smarsh (2018)
- *Restoring Opportunity* by Greg J. Duncan and Richard J. Murnane (2014)
- *Scarcity: Why Having Too Little Means So Much* by Sendhil Mullainathan and Eldar Shafir (2014)
- *Slow Violence and the Environmentalism of the Poor* by Rob Nixon (2011)
- *Toxic Inequality* by Thomas M. Shapiro (2017)
- *The Unwinding* by George Packer (2013)

Key Terms: A DEI Glossary

Another very useful tool outside of the text or book recommendations I've provided is the key DEI terms and concepts. Within this chapter, I provide an excerpt of an entire DEI glossary that is incredibly comprehensive in order to cover a variety of concepts.

This glossary comes from the National Association of Counties (NACo) for Diversity, Equity, and Inclusion (https://tinyurl.com/2s38rmnk).

Ableism   A belief or set of discriminatory actions against individuals with physical or intellectual disabilities or psychiatric disorders.

Accessibility   The intentional design or redesign of physical spaces, technology, policies, system, entity products, and services (to name a few) that increase one's ability to use, access, and obtain the respective element.

Accommodation   A change in the environment or in the way things are customarily done that enables an individual with a disability to have equal opportunity, access, and participation.

Accomplice   A person who knowingly, voluntarily, intentionally, or directly challenges institutionalized racism, colonization, and white supremacy by blocking or impeding racist people, policies, and structures. The actions of an accomplice are coordinated, and they work to disrupt the status quo and challenge systems of oppression.

Acculturation   The process of learning and incorporating the language, values, beliefs, and behaviors that make up a distinct culture. This concept is not to be confused with assimilation, in which an individual or group may give up certain aspects of its culture to adapt to that of the prevailing culture. Under the process of acculturation, an individual will adopt new practices while still retaining their distinct culture.

ADA   An acronym that stands for the Americans with Disabilities Act. The ADA is a civil rights law signed in 1990 that prohibits discrimination against people with disabilities.

Affirm   To acknowledge, respect, and support a person's identity regarding race, ethnicity, sexual orientation, gender identity, experiences, ideas, or beliefs or encouraging the development of an individual.

Affirmative action   Proactive policies and procedures for remedying the effect of past discrimination and ensuring the implementation of equal employment and educational opportunities for recruiting, hiring, training, and promoting women, minorities, people with disabilities, and veterans in compliance with the federal requirements enforced by the Office of Federal Contract Compliance Programs (OFCCP).

Ageism   Prejudiced thoughts and discriminatory actions based on differences in age; usually that of younger persons against older.

Ally   Someone who makes the commitment and effort to recognize their privilege (based on gender, class, race, sexual identity, etc.) and work in solidarity with oppressed groups in the struggle for justice. An ally recognizes that though they are not a member of a marginalized group(s) they support, they make a concentrated effort to better understand the struggle of another's circumstances. An ally may have more privilege and recognize that privilege in society.

ANNH   An acronym that stands for Alaska Native and Native Hawaiian Serving Institutions. These are institutions of higher learning in which 20% or more of the student demographics are Native Alaskans and 10% or more are Native Hawaiians.

Anti-racism   Refers to the work of actively opposing discrimination based on race by advocating for changes in political, economic, and social life.

Assimilation   The process by which an individual of a minority group gradually adopts characteristics of the majority culture, thereby becoming a member of that culture. This can include the adoption of language, culinary tastes, interpersonal communication, gender roles, and style of dress. Assimilation can be voluntary or forced.

Belonging   A sense of being secure, recognized, affirmed, and accepted equally such that full participation is possible.

Bias (prejudice)   An inclination or preference, especially one that interferes with impartial judgment. A form of prejudice that results from the universal tendency and need of individuals to classify others into categories.

Bigotry   An unreasonable or irrational attachment to negative stereotypes and prejudices.

BIPoC   An acronym that stands for Black, Indigenous and People of Color. It is based on the recognition of collective experiences of systemic racism and meant to emphasize the hardships faced by Black and Indigenous people in the United States and Canada and is also meant to acknowledge that not all People of Color face the same levels of injustice. The use of this term is still evolving and contested by some activists.

Bystander   A person who is present at an event or incident but does not take part in, redirect, stop, or otherwise affect the event or incident.

Chicano/a   A term adopted by some Mexican Americans to demonstrate pride in their heritage, born out of the national Chicano movement that was politically aligned with the civil rights movement to end racial oppression and social inequalities of Mexican Americans. Chicano pertains to the experience of Mexican-descended individuals living in the United States. Not all Mexican Americans identify as Chicano.

Cisgender/cis   A term for people whose self-perceived gender identity aligns with their assigned sex at birth. The term *cisgender* can also be shortened to *cis*.

Classism   The institutional, cultural, and individual set of actions and beliefs that assign differential value to people according to their socioeconomic status.

Code-switching   The conscious or unconscious act of altering one's communication style and/or appearance depending on the specific situation of whom one is speaking to, what is being discussed, and the relationship and power and/or community dynamics between those involved. Often members of the non-dominant group code-switch to minimize the impact of bias from the dominant group.

Colonization   The action or process of settling among and establishing control over the Indigenous people of an area that can begin as geographical intrusion in the form of agricultural, urban, or industrial encroachments. The result of such incursion is the dispossession of vast amounts of lands from the original inhabitants. The dispossession of lands is often legalized after the fact resulting in institutionalized inequality that becomes a permanent fixture of society.

Color-blind racial ideology   The attitude that people should be treated as equally as possible, without regard to race or ethnicity. Though seemingly equitable, it tends to overlook the importance of people's cultures and the manifestations of racism in policy or institutions.

Colorism   The prejudice and or discrimination against an individual with darker skin color, tone, shade, pigmentation, or complexion.

Critical race theory (CRT)   A school of thought that acknowledges that racism exists within US social institutions, systems, laws, regulations, and procedures and produces differential outcomes. CRT explores and critiques American history from this race-based perspective as a way to openly talk about how the country's history has an effect on our society and institutions today.

Cultural appropriation   The act of adopting or stealing cultural elements (e.g., icons, rituals, aesthetic standards, or behavior) of one culture or subculture by another for personal use or profit. It is generally applied when the subject culture is a minority culture. Often occurs without any real understanding of why the original (or "appropriated") culture took part in these activities.

Cultural competence   The ability of an individual or organization to understand how inequity can be (and has been) perpetuated through socialized behaviors and using that knowledge to disrupt inequitable practices; the ability to function effectively and empathetically as an individual and/or as an organization within the context of the cultural beliefs, behaviors, and needs presented by another's culture.

Cultural humility   An interpersonal stance that is open to individuals and different cultural communities and experiences in relation to aspects of one's own cultural identity. Maintaining cultural humility requires learning and understanding the complexity of identities and how they evolve over time.

Cultural identity   The identity or feeling of belonging to a group based on nationality, ethnicity, religion, social class, generation, locality, or other types of social groups with their own distinct culture.

Culture   A social system of customs, behaviors, and norms that a group of people develops to ensure its survival and adaptation. It is also a system of values, habits, skills, ideologies, and beliefs.

Damage imagery   Visual, text/narrative, or data used to highlight inequities presented without appropriate historical and sociopolitical context. Damage imagery can be corrected by explaining systemic and historical barriers and focusing on solutions within the communities that are the subject of the visuals, text/narratives, or data.

Deadnaming   Using a person's birth name or name they used previously rather than their current chosen name.

Disability   The physical or mental condition, the perception of a physical or mental impairment, or a history of having had a physical or mental impairment that can affect an individual's life in one or more major life activities.

Discrimination   The unequal and unfair treatment of individuals or groups based on race, gender, social class, sexual orientation, physical ability, religion, national origin, age, intellectual or mental abilities, and other categories that may result in differences. It also describes the act of making unjustified distinctions between certain social or racial groups or classes.

Distributional equity   Programs, policies, and practices that result in a fair distribution of benefits and burdens across all segments of a community, prioritizing those with highest need.

Dominant group   The group within a society with the power, privilege, and social status that controls and defines societal resources and social, political, and economic systems and norms.

Equality   In the context of diversity, equality is typically defined as treating everyone the same and giving everyone access to the same opportunities. It means each individual or group of people is given the same resources or opportunities.

ESL   An acronym for English as a second language. ESL refers to individuals who do not speak English as their first or primary language but may still be proficient in speaking English.

Ethnicity   A common identity based on ancestry, language, culture, nation, or region of origin. Ethnic groups can possess shared attributes, including religion, beliefs, customs, and/or shared memories and experiences.

Feminism   The theory and practice that focuses on the advocacy of social, economic, and political equality among men, women, and all gender identities.

Gender expression   The way in which a person embodies or demonstrates their gender outwardly through the ways they act, dress, behave, interact, or other perceived characteristics. Society identifies these cues as masculine or feminine, although what is considered masculine or feminine changes over time and varies by culture. *See also* Gender identity.

Gender identity   Simply put, gender identity refers to how a person sees themselves in terms of their gender. That is, it refers to a person's own internal sense of self and their gender, whether that is man, woman, neither, or both. Unlike gender expression, gender identity is not outwardly visible to others.

(Personal) gender pronouns (PGPs)   The set of pronouns that an individual personally uses and would like others to use when referring to them. There are several types of personal pronouns used for different groups and identities including gendered, gender neutral, and gender inclusive. Although the list of personal pronouns is continuously evolving, the intention of using a person's pronouns correctly is to reduce the adverse societal effects of those with personal pronouns that don't match their perceived gender identity.

Gentrification   A process of economic change in a historically disinvested neighborhood that happens through mechanisms such as real estate investment and increase in higher-income residents, resulting in the displacement of long-term residents and demographic changes in income, education, and racial makeup.

Harassment   Unwanted conduct with the purpose or effect of violating the dignity of a person and creating an intimidating, hostile, degrading, humiliating, or offensive environment based on their race, color, sex, sexual orientation, religion, national origin, disability, and/or age, among other things.

HBCU   An acronym that stands for historically Black colleges and universities.

Hispanic   A term that describes people, descendants, and cultures of Spanish-speaking countries, including many Latin American countries and Spain. The term is not synonymous with Latino/Latina/Latinx. *See also* Latinx.

Homophobia   Fear, prejudice, discomfort, or hatred of people attracted to members of the same gender. It occurs in a wide social context that systematically disadvantages LGBTQ+ people and promotes and rewards anti-LGBTQ+ sentiment.

Health equity   Means that everyone has a fair and just opportunity to be as healthy as possible. This requires removing obstacles to health such as poverty, discrimination, and their consequences, including powerlessness and lack of access to good jobs with fair pay, quality education and housing, safe environments, and health care.

HSI   An acronym that stands for Hispanic-serving institutions. These are eligible institutions of higher education with an enrollment rate of 25% or higher of Hispanic undergraduate full-time equivalent students.

IFL   An acronym that stands for identity first language, which positions disability as an identity category and central to a person's sense of self. In IFL, the identifying word comes first in the sentence and highlights the person's embrace of their identity. Examples could be "autistic person" or "Deaf individual." *See also* PFL.

Implicit bias (hidden or unconscious bias)   The unconscious attitudes or stereotypes that affect a person's understanding, actions, or decisions as they relate to people from different groups.

Imposter syndrome   The fear that some high-achieving individuals have of being exposed as a fraud or inadequate, inhibiting their ability to recognize their own accomplishments, common in members of underrepresented groups.

Inclusive language   Language that acknowledges diversity, conveys respect to all people, is sensitive to differences, and promotes equal opportunities.

Indigenous people   A term used to identify ethnic groups who are the earliest known inhabitants of an area (also known as First People) in contrast to groups that have settled, occupied, or colonized the area more recently. In the United States, this can refer to groups traditionally termed Native Americans (American Indians), Alaska Natives, and Native Hawaiians. In Canada, it can refer to the groups typically termed First Nations.

Individual racism   Individual or personal beliefs, assumptions, attitudes, and actions that perpetuate or support racism. Individual racism can occur at both a conscious and unconscious level and can be active or passive. Examples can include avoiding people of color and accepting or approving of racist acts or jokes. *See also* Racism.

Institutional racism   Unfair or biased institutional or organizational practices and policies that create different (or inequitable) outcomes for different racial groups. These policies may not specifically target any racial group but may create advantages for some groups and oppression or disadvantages for others. Examples can include policies within the criminal justice system that punish People of Color more than their white counterparts, or within the workforce system in which hiring practices can significantly disadvantaged workers of color. *See also* Individual racism, Structural racism, and Systemic racism.

Internalized racism   The conscious or unconscious development of ideas, beliefs, social structures, actions, and behaviors that confirm one's acceptance of the dominant society's racist tropes and stereotypes about their own race. It is the simultaneous hating of oneself and one's own race and valuing the dominant race.

Intersectionality   The intertwining of social identities such as gender, race, ethnicity, social class, religion, sexual orientation, or gender identity, which result in unique experiences, opportunities, barriers, or social inequality.

Justice   The process of society moving from an unfair, unequal, or inequitable state to one that is fair, equal, or equitable. A transformative practice that relies on the entire community to acknowledge past and current harms to reform societal morals and subsequently the governing laws. Proactive enforcement of policies, practices, and attitudes that produce equitable access, opportunities, treatment, and outcomes for all regardless of the various identities that one holds.

Latinx   A gender-neutral or nonbinary term that refers to a person of Latin American origin or descent (gender-neutral version of Latino or Latina).

LGBT/LGBTQ/LGBTQIA+   Acronyms that refer to communities of individuals who are not heterosexual and/or cisgender. Individually, the letters stand for lesbian, gay, bisexual, transgender, queer, intersex, asexual, pansexual. The plus (+) includes all other expressions of gender identity and sexual orientation and recognizes that definitions may grow and evolve over time.

Marginalization   The process that occurs when members of a dominant group relegate a particular group (minority groups and cultures) to the edge of society by not allowing them an active voice, identity, or place for the purpose of maintaining power. Marginalized groups have restricted access to resources such as education and health care for achieving their aims.

Microaggression   Commonplace daily verbal, behavioral, or environmental indignities, whether intentional or unintentional, which communicate hostile, derogatory slights toward culturally marginalized groups.

Misgender   Referring or relating to a person using language, whether a word or a pronoun, that is not in line with another's gender identity, whether intentionally or unintentionally. This behavior or action often occurs when people make assumptions about a person's gender identity.

Minority group   Any group of people who, because of their physical, neurological, or cultural characteristics, are singled out from others in society through differential and unequal treatment, and who therefore regard themselves as objects of collective discrimination. The dominant group is that which holds the most power in society compared to minority groups. Being a numerical minority is not a characteristic of being in a minority group; it is the lack of power that is the predominant characteristic of a minority group.

Misogyny   Hatred, aversion, or prejudice against women. Misogyny can be manifested in numerous ways, including sexual discrimination, denigration of women, violence against women, and sexual objectification of women.

Misogynoir   An extreme form of sexism rooted in racism. The term describes contempt for or ingrained prejudice toward Black women. The unique oppression experienced by Black women due to the intersectionality of gender, race, class, and sexual orientation combined with discrimination. Misogynoir uses and reinforces stereotypes of Black women.

Multiculturalism   The practice of acknowledging, respecting, and supporting the various cultures, religions, languages, social equity, races, ethnicities, attitudes, and opinions within an environment or involving a cultural or ethnic group. The theory and practice promote the peaceful coexistence of all identities and people.

NASNTI   An acronym that stands for Native American Indian serving, non-tribal institutions. These are institutions of higher learning in which 10% or more of the student demographics are Native American and the institution does qualify as a tribal college and university (TCU).

Neurodiversity   Neurological differences that present in the way individuals act, think, hear, and communicate. These differences in neurological conditions can include dyspraxia, dyslexia, attention deficit hyperactivity disorder, dyscalculia, autism spectrum, and more.

Nonbinary   A term describing a spectrum of gender identities that are not exclusively male or female. Nonbinary people may identify outside the gender binary categories.

Oppression   A system of supremacy and discrimination for the benefit of a limited dominant group perpetuated through differential or unjust treatment, ideology, and institutional control.

Othering   The perception or intentional/unintentional placement of a group in contrast to the societal norm; the identifying of a group as a threat to the favored dominant group.

Patriarchy   Actions and beliefs that prioritize men in systems and positions of power and social society and privilege. Patriarchy may be practiced systemically in the ways and methods through which power is distributed in society or it may simply influence how individuals interact with one another interpersonally.

PBI   An acronym that stands for predominantly Black institutions. These are institutions of higher learning in which 40% or more of the student demographics are Black.

People of color   A collective term for individuals of Asian, African, Latinx, and Native American backgrounds with the common experience of being targeted and oppressed by racism. Although each oppressed group is affected by racism differently and maintains its own unique identity and culture, there is also the recognition that racism has the potential to unite oppressed people in a collective of resistance. For this reason, many individuals who identify as members of racially oppressed groups also claim the identity of being People of Color. This in no way diminishes their specific cultural or racial identity; rather, it is an affirmation of the multiple layers of identity of every individual.

PFL   An acronym that stands for person-first language, which conveys respect by emphasizing that people with disabilities are first and foremost people. The most common example is "person with a disability." *See also* IFL.

Power   The ability to exercise one's will over others. Power occurs when some individuals or groups wield a greater advantage over others, thereby allowing them greater access to and control over resources. Wealth, whiteness, citizenship, patriarchy, heterosexism, and education are a few key social mechanisms through which power operates.

Prejudice   An inclination or preference, especially one that interferes with impartial judgment and can be rooted in stereotypes that deny the right of individual members of certain groups to be recognized and treated as individuals with unique characteristics.

Privilege   An unearned, sustained advantage afforded to some over others based on group identities related to race, gender, sexuality, ability, socioeconomic status, age, and/or other identities.

Procedural equity   An examination of procedural rights that includes authentic engagement through an inclusive and accessible development and implementation of fair programs or policies.

PWIs   An acronym that stands for predominantly white institutions. These are institutions of higher learning in which 50% or more of the student demographics are white.

Race   A social construct that divides people into distinct groups based on characteristics such as physical appearance (particularly skin color), ancestral heritage, cultural affiliation, cultural history, ethnic classification, and, often, are associated with the social, economic, and political needs of a society at a given time.

Racial anxiety   The concerns that often arise both before and during interracial interactions. People of color experience racial anxiety when they worry that they will be subject to discriminatory treatment. White people, however, experience it when they worry that they will be perceived as racist.

Racial disparity   The imbalances and incongruities between the treatment of racial groups, including economic status, income, housing options, societal treatment, safety, and many other aspects of life and society. Contemporary and past discrimination in the United States, and globally, has profoundly affected the inequalities seen in society today. *See also* Racial equity and Racial justice.

Racial equity   Means race is no longer a predictor of outcomes, generally because of more equitable policies, practices, attitudes, and cultural messages. That is, racial equity refers to what a genuinely non-racist society would look like. In a racially equitable society, the distribution of society's benefits and burdens would not be skewed by race. Racial equity demands that we pay attention not just to individual-level discrimination but also to overall social outcomes. *See also* Racial justice.

Racial justice The systematic fair treatment of people of all races, resulting in equitable opportunities and outcomes for all. Racial justice is not just the absence of discrimination and inequities but also the presence of deliberate systems and supports to achieve and sustain racial equity through proactive and preventative measures. *See also* Racial equity.

Racism The systematic subjugation of members of targeted racial groups, generally non-white groups, who hold less sociopolitical power. It involves actions correlated with or resulting from bigotry or the thinking that one's racial differences produce an inherent inferiority of a particular race, usually the dominant race. Racism differs from prejudice, hatred, or discrimination because it requires one racial group to have systematic power and superiority over other groups in society.

Racially coded language Language that is seemingly race neutral but is a disguise for racial stereotypes without the stigma of explicit racism.

Safe space An environment where everyone feels comfortable expressing themselves and participating fully, without fear of attack, ridicule, or denial of experience (i.e., a judgment-free zone).

Sexual orientation The sex(es) or gender(s) to whom a person is emotionally, physically, sexually, and/or romantically attracted. Examples of sexual orientation can include gay, lesbian, bisexual, heterosexual, asexual, pansexual, queer, and so on.

Social justice A form of activism based on principles of equity and inclusion that encompasses a vision of society in which the distribution of resources is equitable, and all members are physically and psychologically safe and secure.

Social self-view An individual's perception about which social identity group(s) they belong to.

SOGIE An acronym that honors the fluidity of numerous and ever-expanding identities related to sexual orientation (SO), gender identity (GI), and (gender) expression (E). *See also* Sexual orientation, Gender identity and Gender expression.

Stereotype A form of generalization rooted in blanket beliefs and false assumptions; a product of categorization processes that can result in a prejudiced attitude, uncritical judgment, and intentional or unintentional discrimination. Stereotypes are typically negative and based on little information that does not recognize individualism and personal agency.

Structural equity The identification and removal of institutional barriers to fair and equal opportunities with recognition to historical, cultural, and institutional dynamics and structures that routinely advantage privileged groups in society and result in chronic, cumulative disadvantage for subordinated groups.

Structural inequality Systemic disadvantage(s) of one social group compared to other groups, rooted, and perpetuated through discriminatory practices (conscious or unconscious) and reinforced through institutions, ideologies, representations, policies/laws, and practices. Structural inequality thus refers to the system of privilege and inequality created, designed, and maintained by interlocking societal institutions.

Structural racism The overarching system of racial bias across institutions and society. It is a system in which public policies, institutional practices, cultural representations, and other norms work in various, often reinforcing ways to perpetuate racial inequities. It encompasses dimensions of our history and culture that have allowed privileges associated with "whiteness" and disadvantages associated with "color" to endure and adapt over time. Examples can include the racial gap in wealth, homeownership, education, historical redlining practices, among other factors. *See also* Individual racism, Institutional racism, and Systemic racism.

Systemic racism　An interlocking and reciprocal relationship among the individual, institutional, and structural levels that function as a system of racism. These various levels of racism operate together in a lockstep model and function together as a whole system: (1) individual (within interactions between people), (2) institutional (within institutions and systems of power), and (3) structural or societal (among institutions and across society). In many ways *systemic racism* and *structural racism* are synonymous. If there is a difference between the terms, it can be said to exist in the fact that a structural racism analysis pays more attention to the historical, cultural, and social psychological aspects of our currently racialized society. *See also* Individual Racism, Institutional racism, and Structural racism.

Targeted universalism　An approach to equity work that sets universal goals followed by targeted processes to achieve said goals. Within a targeted universalism framework, universal goals are set for all individuals and groups. The strategies developed to achieve the goals are targeted based on how different groups are situated within structures, culture, and across geographies to obtain the universal goal.

TCU　An acronym that stands for tribal colleges and universities. These are institutions of higher learning in which 50% or more of the student demographics are Native American, Inuit, or Alaska Native.

Transgender　An umbrella term for people whose gender identity and/or gender expression differs from their sex assigned at birth. *Trans* is sometimes used as shorthand for transgender. Transgender or *trans* does not imply any form of sexual orientation. Cisgender is a gender identity in which an individual's self-perception of their gender matches their sex. *See also* Cisgender, Gender identity, and Gender expression.

Trans-misogyny　The negative attitudes expressed through cultural hate, individual and state violence, and discrimination directed toward trans women and transfeminine people. Additionally, trans-misogyny is the intersection of transphobia and misogyny. *See also* Misogyny.

Transphobia　Fear or hatred of transgender people; transphobia is manifested in many ways, including violence, harassment, and discrimination. This phobia can exist in LGBTQIA+ and straight communities.

Underrepresented groups　Groups who traditionally (or historically) have not had equal access to economic opportunities because of discrimination or other societal barriers. This may vary by context and geography but can include race, gender, ethnicity, sexual orientation, disability, or low-income status. Examples of groups that may be considered underrepresented can include women or women of color in a traditionally male and/or white discipline such as science, technology, engineering, and mathematics.

Veteran status　Whether an individual has served in a nation's armed forces (or other uniformed services).

White fragility　The state in which even a minimum amount of racial stress becomes intolerable, triggering a range of defensive moves in white people. These moves include the outward display of emotions such as anger, fear, and guilt, and behaviors such as argumentation, silence, and leaving the stress-inducing situation. These behaviors, in turn, function to reinstate white racial equilibrium. Racial stress results from an interruption to what is racially familiar.

White privilege The inherent set of advantages, entitlements, benefits, and choices bestowed on people solely because they are white; an exemption of social, political, and/or economic burdens placed on non-white people. Generally, white people who experience privilege, both at the collective and individual level, do so without being conscious of it and may not experience socioeconomic privilege but are not hindered by the economic barriers associated with the color of one's skin.

White supremacy The idea (or ideology) that white people and the ideas, thoughts, beliefs, and actions of white people are superior to People of Color and their ideas, thoughts, beliefs, and actions. White supremacy is ever present in our institutional and cultural assumptions that assign value, morality, goodness, and humanity to the white group while casting people and communities of color as worthless (worth less), immoral, bad, and inhuman and "undeserving." *See also* White privilege.

Xenophobia Any attitude, behavior, practice, or policy that explicitly or implicitly reflects the belief that immigrants are inferior to the dominant group of people. Xenophobia is reflected in interpersonal, institutional, and systemic levels of oppression and white supremacy.

References

INTRODUCTION

Najarron, I. (2022). K-12 Diversity, equity, and inclusion trainings: Are they divisive or effective? *EducationWeek* (March 4). https://www.edweek.org/leadership/k-12-diversity-equity-and-inclusion-trainings-are-they-divisive-or-effective/2022/03

CHAPTER 2

Love, B. J. (2020). Developing a liberatory conscience. In M. Adams, W. J. Blumenfeld, H. W. Hackman, M. L. Peters, & X. Zuniga (Eds.), *Readings for Diversity and Social Justice*. Routledge.

Dismantling Racism (2016). 2016 Workbook. https://resourcegeneration.org/wp-content/uploads/2018/01/2016-dRworks-workbook.pdf

Diversity in the Classroom, UCLA Diversity & Faculty Development (2014). https://equity.ucla.edu/wp-content/uploads/2016/06/DiversityintheClassroom2014Web.pdf

CHAPTER 5

Khalifa, M. A., Gooden, M. A., & Davis, J. E. (2016). Culturally responsive school leadership: A synthesis of the literature. *Review of Educational Research*, *86*(4), 1272–1311. https://doi.org/10.3102/0034654316630383

CHAPTER 6

Dixon, B. (2010). When reforming educations means destroying communities. *HuffPost*. https://www.huffpost.com/entry/when-reforming-education_b_530799

Bohnet, I. (2016, April 18). How to take the bias out of interviews. *Harvard Business Review*. https://hbr.org/2016/04/how-to-take-the-bias-out-of-interviews

Acknowledgments

Thank you to my immediate family (my husband, parents, siblings, grandparents, in-laws, aunts, uncles, and cousins) and every peer, friend, mentor, colleague, and supporter I've met in my life who has helped me recognize, nurture, and embrace my gifts; helped me accept and love myself; and helped me to advance social change—no matter what it cost me along the way. I have always known that I am a bridger, called to link divides and drive justice and positive change. However, I have not always trusted myself along the journey of becoming who I am today. I stand grateful to every positive and negative experience I've ever faced as they have all served a mighty purpose of working for my ultimate good. Every season and chapter of our lives holds purpose, and in publishing this book, I realize that every personal and professional season and chapter of my life has led me to be equipped inwardly to produce *What Goes Unspoken*.

As a woman of faith, I am incredibly thankful to God for providing this opportunity to bridge gaps and divides, to heal, and to positively change schools, systems, educators, children, families, nonprofits, and companies across the world.

About the Author

A native of historic Selma, Alabama, Krystal Hardy Allen is the founder and CEO of K. Allen Consulting (www.kallenconsulting.org), an award-winning former teacher and principal, and a respected DEI thought leader. Krystal began her career teaching elementary school, then moving into instructional leadership as an administrator (i.e., SPED coordinator, assistant principal, and then principal), and in 2017, became a social entrepreneur founding what has become a highly sought-after international education and management consulting firm serving more than eight countries; major corporate brands, such as Amazon and Microsoft; and public and private school systems, small businesses, nonprofits, and government agencies. Most recently featured within *Time* magazine for her thought leadership on racial bias with K–12 classrooms, she is a 2019 Gambit 40 Under 40 recipient, a 2019 Aspen Institute Ideas Festival Scholar, the 2016 Urban League of Louisiana Activist Award recipient. Krystal was also named one of the 2022 Most Influential Women in Business in Louisiana by the BRM Regional Chamber of Commerce and serves on the board of directors for several national and state nonprofit organizations that advance educational equity. A first-generation college graduate, Krystal earned her BA from the University of Notre Dame, MEd from NLU-Chicago, and is currently undergoing doctoral studies in K–12 Urban Educational Leadership at Teachers College, Columbia University. Krystal's work—be it customized professional development workshops, strategic planning, leadership coaching, and thought leadership—centers DEI, social justice, adult learning, and organizational development.

Index